cooking with an accent

AN IMMIGRATION LAWYER'S COOKBOOK

7-21-06

to Barbara

cook away!

Mira

Linh Trieu

BY MIRA MDIVANI

PHOTOGRAPHY BY ELIZABETH COOK
DESIGN BY LINH TRIEU

Author: Mira Mdivani
Photography: Beth Cook
Design: Linh Trieu

Copyright © 2005 Mira Mdivani

Published in 2005 by Vertex Press, Kansas City, Missouri, USA

Editors: Lisa Rausch, Grant Wallace, Linh Trieu, Maria Iliakova, George Vial

LIBRARY OF CONGRESS CATALOGING-IN-PUBLICATION DATA
Mdivani, Mira
Cooking with an Accent, An Immigration Lawyer's Cookbook

ISBN 0-9774524-1-7

Printed in the United States of America by Harvest Graphics

To my daughter Maria Iliakova

table of contents

acknowledgements 2

recipes 3

table of contents

recipes

acknowledgements

This book is truly a joint effort, and I need to say thanks to all involved. First, all the cooks and their families - my clients and friends, clients who became friends, and friends who from time to time ask me questions about immigration law: all those who gave me recipes and showed up at my house on short notice to cook with me over four hot summer weekends in 2004. You opened your hearts to this project, and encouraged me with your generosity and kindness.

Thanks go to Dr. Ninfa Indacochea-Redmond, Susan and Alex Masson, Jamie and Steven Stone, Marwan Chebaro, Rebekah Moses and Pablo Marin, Natalia and Sergei Bautin, Felecia and Francis Kasi, Wendy and Martin Rudderforth, Karina and Igor Papikian, Natalia Golovko Butler and Pastor Brian Butler, Leon and Heather Versfeld, Melissa and Juan Castillo, Anand Nagarajan and Miryana Lazarevic, Liliya and Vladimir Kutateladze, Yelena and Vladimir Logashov, Ramaswamy Subramanyam and Gayathri Ramaswamy, Stanislav Ioudenitch and Tatiana Kouznetsova, Pastor Jorge Herlein and Ester Paccot, Kathy and Laurent Denis, Chithra and Mahadevan Puliadi, Simran and Michael Nutter, Rita Witt and Bill Capotosto, Steven and Nancy Dobson, Svetlana and Grant Topchiev, Linh Trieu and George Vial, Tien Bui, Leyla and Jim McMullen, Esther Galmarini, Melinda and Kori Lewis, Sue Storm, Dr. Monica Mingucci, Allyson and Sergio Gonzalez, Vesna Jokic, Amber Hamilton and Abel Rivera, Penny Porter Brosoto and Amiel Brosoto, and Maria Varchavtchik Imhoff and Michael Imhoff.

Second, I am grateful to Beth Cook for her talent and patience: shooting pictures for 12 hours a day in my tiny living room, with 20 people in the house, each wanting the food to look just so, was not the easiest task in the world. She took pictures full of life, and they make me hungry! Beth, I am excited that you chose to do your first book with me, and wish you a wonderful future in photography.

Third, thanks to Linh Trieu for her creativity and understanding. Not being a cook or a cookbook writer, and knowing nothing about the creative process, I kept coming up with grandioso ideas and kept changing my mind. Linh transformed it all into a book, I simply do not know how, and we managed to become friends over it, which is an even better achievement, as far as I am concerned. Special thanks to George Vial, who came up with the title and helped with editing, and to Trinh Trieu who helped with everything while we were shooting, from taking snapshots to washing the dishes in the kitchen.

I am thankful to my daughter Maria Iliakova who jump-started the publishing of the book after pictures, stories and recipes had sat in a box for almost a year because I could never make it my first priority: you see, clients' cases are always more important. Maria kept giving me deadlines, sending e-mails, and having fights with me over the cookbook. Eventually we figured out we couldn't work together because we spent more time fighting than working, and the publishing was completed without Maria, but had she not pushed me hard, there would have been no book at all. Thank you, Maria.

I am also very thankful to Lisa Rausch and Grant Wallace, legal assistants at the Mdivani Law Firm, for their invaluable assistance editing this book. They made many excellent suggestions, told me many times to re-write paragraphs because they "do not make sense," and pretty much put their heart and soul into making the book read well. As for Grant, he even went as far as cooking recipes again after we wrote them down. What can I say: the rest of the world can only envy me because I am fortunate to work with Lisa and Grant on a daily basis.

A big thank you to my family: my husband Dennis Ayzin, my dad Archil Mdivani, and my son Alexey and daughter Maria, for their patience while we occupied the house cooking, setting up pictures, sweating under the lighting equipment, eating, and piling up dirty dishes in the kitchen. At the same time, I have to say, it is not like they did not enjoy all the food and the delightful people they met, so maybe it was more of an adventure on their part than sacrifice, but I am thankful anyway.

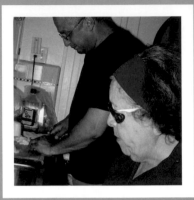

STARTERS

PICTURED FROM TOP, LEFT TO RIGHT: *Ham Rolls; Archil Mdivani inspecting his grapevines; Steven Dobson; Tomato and Cilantro; Wendy and Martin Rudderforth; Marwin Chebaro and Ninfa Indacochea-Redmond; Poori and Potato Masala; Archil Mdivani and Chithra Puliadi; Mira Mdivani.*

My family enjoys this summer salad when we can get "good" tomatoes from the River Market in downtown Kansas City, with fresh cheese and crusty bread. Like my family, the salad is a little from everywhere: some of it is from Russia, some from Georgia, some from Uzbekistan, some from Greece and Italy (in my imagination only), but all of it from my new home, America.

Mira's Summer Salad

by Mira Mdivani

Place lettuce leaves on a large plate. Begin layering your salad. First, place tomatoes on lettuce leaves. Sprinkle with salt and pepper. Next, layer with cucumbers, peppers, and onions. Sprinkle with vinegar and oil. Top with basil and cilantro. Serve with feta cheese, kalamata olives and some good bread.

4 large tomatoes *sliced*

4 small cucumbers *peeled and sliced*

1 head green leaf lettuce

4 sweet banana peppers *cored and sliced*

1 medium onion *thinly sliced*

a handful of fresh, sweet basil *roughly chopped*

a handful of fresh cilantro *very finely chopped*

3 tbsp olive oil

1 tbsp white vinegar

salt and pepper *to taste*

When I come home, *I usually set the table for dinner and tell my husband about my day. I am careful not to disclose names of my clients. Dennis knows not to discuss this with anyone else. Sometimes I am delighted to tell him that a really tough case is over.*

I tell him how my client from Honduras finally got his green card after 14 years of waiting in limbo and how this big macho guy had tears in his eyes when he was told he was being granted permanent residency in this country. Or I tell Dennis that I am done with a big I-9 audit and employer immigration compliance project. Or I tell him about a nice naturalization case. On many other occasions, I tell Dennis how fired up I am because of the injustice done to my clients, both American and foreign.

I tell him about husbands, wives and children who are separated for years because our law does not provide for a sufficient number of family immigrant visas. I tell him about employers trying to obtain appropriate work visas for their foreign employees only to find out that all allocated visas are used up! My husband often tells me that I should write a book about it all.

But...while I am writing that book, who will be taking care of my clients? So instead, I decided I would do something simpler: a cookbook. I asked my clients and friends to come to my house to cook with me. I also asked Linh Trieu to help with the book design and editing. Linh brought her friend Elizabeth Cook, a talented photographer, to take pictures. We cooked, ate, took pictures, recorded recipes and stories from all over the world, literally from Singapore and Peru to Great Bend, Kansas. We had a good time and I still haven't lost the weight I gained while we cooked for this book!

Seafood Empanadas al Horno

DOUGH

1-1/2 cups all-purpose flour

1/2 tsp salt

1/2 tsp baking powder

1/4 cup lard or unsalted butter

1/8 cup vegetable shortening

1/4 cup warm water

FILLING

6 garlic cloves *minced*

1/2 cup scallions *chopped*

juice of 2 limes (1/3 cup)

1-1/2 cup mushrooms *diced*

1/2 lb shrimp

1/2 scallops

1 tbsp oil

Makes 8 large or 24 small empanadas.

by Wendy and Martin Rudderforth

Dough
Put the flour, salt and baking powder in a food processor and pulse for 5 seconds. Then add the lard and shortening and process until the mixture looks like coarse meal, about 15 seconds. With the machine running, pour the water through the feed tube in a steady stream and process until dough almost comes together into a ball. Remove dough from the bowl, knead a few times and let it rest for 30 minutes covered with a damp cloth.

Filling
Heat the tablespoon of oil in a pan and sauté the garlic in the oil until translucent. Add the mushrooms and sauté for one more minute. Add shrimp and scallops, lime juice and a pinch of salt. When shrimp begins to turn pink, add scallions and add salt and pepper to taste. Cool filling and drain.

Preparation
Place the dough on a lightly floured surface. Cut it into 2 pieces and roll each piece into a log. Cut each log into 4 rounds, and with a lightly floured rolling pin, roll one round at a time into a circle about 5 inches in diameter. Place two tablespoons of filling into the center of each circle, fold it in half, and press firmly to seal the edges. Trim and crimp the edge with a fork and then pierce the top with the fork to allow steam to escape during baking. Bake on upper oven rack until golden, about 20 minutes. Eat steaming hot or warm.

Wendy and Martin *recently opened Pangea Café and Market in Kansas City, Missouri, where they woo their customers with the world's fare: anything from kebabs, paninis, tabouleh, Pad Thai and tortillas to sushi rolls and of course, empanadas, the dish they cooked for this book. Before Pangea, Wendy attended culinary school at the Art Institute in Los Angeles and worked in prestigious kitchens around Los Angeles and Kansas City. Martin, who is from Argentina, has been in the restaurant business for years, from running the front of the house at Piropos, a great Argentine-style restaurant in Parkville, Missouri, to opening small sushi bars. It looks like their marriage and Pangea Café partnership are the best things for all involved: Kansas City has another super-tasty place to eat while it looks like Martin and Wendy are really enjoying their life and work together. Cheers!*

Puff pastries are widely used throughout South America, where every country has its own specialties when it comes to empanadas (turnovers). In particular, Argentina has a rich variety of these savory pastries. The dough, mostly made with wheat flour and either lard or butter, can contain meat, fowl, seafood, cheese or vegetables as filling: the variations are endless. If you prefer to take a shortcut, you can rely on ready-made puff pastry shells. This recipe is a winner because it tastes delicious and it is also easy to prepare. As a bonus, empanadas freeze beautifully. They are a favorite party appetizer. The best way to eat them is with your hands.

Nova Scotia Mussels

By *Jamie and Steven Stone*

In a tall pot, mix beer (or white wine), 2 tbsp butter, garlic and lemon slices. Bring the contents to a boil, then turn the heat down to a simmer. Add mussels and immediately cover the pot with a lid. Steam for 5-7 minutes, making sure that all shells have opened wide. Discard any shells that remain closed after steaming. Sauté diced bell peppers with 2 tbsp butter until cooked, but still crisp. Sprinkle peppers over mussels and serve with melted butter for dipping.

2 lbs fresh mussels
make sure that all of the shells are tightly closed – don't use any opened ones

1 cup beer or white wine

3 cloves garlic

1/2 lemon
sliced into rounds

4 tbsp butter

1/2 lb yellow, orange and red bell peppers *diced*

Jamie's father was *a member of the Royal Canadian Mountain Police, and the family moved across Canada several times. Summers, however, were always spent at Jamie's grandfather's cottage in Nova Scotia. Mussels were Grandpa's signature dish. When Steven came to meet Jamie's mom, Beverly Anne, and her mom's husband, Jean, in Nova Scotia, the family made mussels. "It represented him joining our family," said Jamie. Jamie's family loves sailing. To their surprise, Steven successfully steered a 40-foot sailboat around buoys and lobster traps during a midnight sail. You could say that Steven's voyage into the family sailed along just as smoothly.*

"We're a family of immigrants," said Jamie, recounting her grandfather's move from Scotland to Nova Scotia. She knew that immigrating to the United States would be a complex process. Even though she is a staunch do-it-yourselfer, Jamie hired a lawyer to handle her immigration. "This was not the time for guesswork," she explained.

Jamie found that grocery stores, a love of which she shares with her mother and sister, are different in the U.S. She explained, "I would spend three hours in stores with 15 different types of mustard. The layout is beautiful!" After moving to the U.S., Jamie learned that instead of Highland dance practices and field hockey tournaments, kids here get involved in cheerleading competitions and baseball games. Despite small differences, she says, "Americans are more similar to us than Canadians think." "Moving here is not a struggle if you are open to it," says Jamie. "When I met Steve in Atlanta, Georgia, he had taught me how to cope with the hot weather. Now that we are moving to New York, I will be teaching him how to cope with the cold."

Russian Potato Salad

6 potatoes

3 carrots

1 onion

5 pickles

2 small fresh cucumbers

1 Granny Smith apple

1 (15 oz) can sweet peas

3 eggs

1 (16 oz) jar light mayonnaise

1/2 lb chicken breast *optional*

By Liliya and Vladimir Kutateladze

Boil potatoes, carrots and eggs. You may also boil chicken if you choose to make this salad with chicken. Remove from water and let cool. Peel and cube the potatoes, carrots, (chicken) and eggs. Dice the apple, onion, pickles and cucumbers. Combine all ingredients, except mayonnaise, in a large bowl. Add salt and pepper to taste. Add the entire jar of mayonnaise into the bowl and mix well. Serve in a large bowl as an appetizer or side dish.

Liliya, Vladimir and *their son Nikoloz came to the United States from Kyrgyzstan. Their grandparents and parents were exiled to Kyrgyzstan under the USSR's communist regime. When the Soviet Union collapsed, people of different ethnicities living in Kyrgyzstan were faced with sorting out harsh realities of the post-Soviet era on their own. Fortunately, the Kutateladze family was granted asylum in this country.*

Several years after their arrival, their son Niloloz speaks English without a trace of an accent. He looks like an all-American boy and especially enjoys football. Liliya and Vladimir had to start their professional lives all over again. Liliya, a dentist with over ten years of experience, can't practice dentistry in the U.S. unless she passes the dentistry board here. She spent several years

learning English and retaking pre-med courses at UMKC while working as a dental assistant, and this year, she began her first year at the UMKC School of Dentistry. Vladimir, who ran a business in Kyrgyzstan, has been working two jobs to put Liliya through dental school again. They are one of the warmest and most gracious families I know. Liliya and Vladimir's determination and strength are an inspiring example to me in my own American journey.

It is not surprising that Liliya chose to cook the Russian Potato Salad for this book. This salad, often called "Olivier" is very popular throughout the former Soviet Union: a holiday table is incomplete without it. There are as many "correct" recipes of this salad as there are cooks. I, of course, have my own version, but I have to keep it to myself until someone asks me to share.

Calamari Salad

By Marwan Chebaro

Separate tentacles from calamari. Slice remaining calamari. Boil water and add tentacles and sliced ginger. Boil for two minutes, then add remaining calamari and boil for another two minutes and drain. Mix remaining ingredients. Add calamari. Toss and serve.

2-1/2 lbs frozen calamari

1-1/2 qt water

2/3 cup lemon juice

1/3 cup olive oil

2-inch piece of ginger
sliced into thin rounds

4 pieces star anise

2-3 banana peppers
seeds removed, sliced

2-3 sweet peppers
seeds removed, sliced

1 cup scallions *finely chopped*

1 handful cilantro
finely chopped

3 tbsp garlic *minced*

1 tbsp ground cumin

1 pinch black pepper

7 pinches kosher salt

2 tbsp paprika

Marwan Chebaro is *a magician! It is impossible to put into words how good his food is. Marwan is from Lebanon, so naturally, he cooks a lot of Lebanese food. But he is also a chef extraordinare who creates amazing improvised dishes, with influences from all over the world. If you want to know what I mean, you should visit Café Rumi, his Kansas City restaurant on 39th and Baltimore.*

The recipe of the Calamari you are reading here is a miracle in itself. Marwan does not write down his recipes. He usually says, "How much? Oh, I don't really know…about six pinches of this and seven pinches of that."

And he cooks so fast! Dr. Ninfa Indacochea-Redmond volunteered to be his scribe while Marwan was busy creating impossible-to-resist aromas in my kitchen. When the Calamari was ready, there were about a dozen people in the house, and we nearly had a fight to see who got to finish it. Make sure you invite your friends to share this delightful, light and exotic dish with you.

TABOULI

5 bunches parsley
finely chopped, stems removed

6 Roma tomatoes *diced*

1 cup scallions

1 cup cracked wheat
*soaked in 1 cup tomato juice or
lemon juice*

1 handful dry mint

5 pinches kosher salt

1 cup olive oil

1/3 cup lemon juice

BATATA KIZBARA

4 large Russet potatoes
cut into 1-inch squares

7 pinches kosher salt

7 pinches ground black pepper

1/3 cup olive oil

1/2 cup cilantro, chopped

1/2 cup lemon juice

5 tbsp garlic *minced*

salt and pepper *to taste*

Tabouli

By Marwan Chebaro

Place all ingredients in a bowl. Toss and serve.

Batata Kizbara

By Marwan Chebaro

Mix potatoes, salt, pepper and olive oil in a bowl, coating the potatoes with the other ingredients. Place the mixture in a shallow baking pan and spread evenly. Bake at 375°-400° F for 45 minutes.

Once potatoes are done, return them to mixing bowl and add cilantro, garlic and lemon juice. Mix well. Salt and pepper to taste.

Not pictured.

See Marwan's story and photo on page 14.

Baku Eggplant

By Karina and Igor Papikian

Cut the ends off of the eggplants and place in salted water for 15 minutes to remove natural bitterness of the eggplant. Squeeze out water. Slice eggplant into 1/8 inch thick slices.

Heat skillet and add olive oil. Fry eggplant on both sides until browned. Sprinkle with salt and pepper, set aside. Pan-fry tomatoes, onions and green peppers with olive oil.

Layer the salad, do not forget a little salt and pepper for each layer. Start with eggplant, then add onions, tomatoes, green peppers and top again with more onion.

Chop cilantro and mince garlic, then sprinkle over vegetables. This salad can be served warm or chilled.

2 medium-sized eggplants

2 large tomatoes *sliced*

1 yellow onion *sliced*

2 green peppers *sliced*

1 cup olive oil

salt and pepper *to taste*

garlic *to taste*

1/2 bunch fresh cilantro

Karina and Igor *are U.S. Citizens of Armenian descent who were born and lived in Baku, Azerbaijan. Their memories of Baku are bitter-sweet: how wonderful it was, how terrible it was. Growing up and going to college, working, making friends, falling in love in a sun-lit, beautiful, loud, tasty, multi-national Baku. Fleeing at night, with the help of Azeri friends, from the Azeri mob killing Armenians in the middle of the winter - scary, chilling Baku.*

The U.S. government granted this family asylum. A U.S. Embassy officer told them on the phone, "You are approved, and you should go to Kansas City." Karina's father Aram Galoyants exclaimed, "Great! Kansas City is the BEST city in the world!" Karina said, "Dad, what are you talking about? What do you know about this place?" Aram replied, "What I know is that Kansas City is the best place in the world because WE are going there!"

That's pretty much the attitude. The family arrived in Kansas City with their suitcases and $350 cash, not knowing a single soul here. Both Karina and Igor used to be engineers in Azerbaijan. Their first jobs in the U.S. were at McDonald's, the one place where they could reach without a car from their apartment on Brownell. It took both of them years to return to

professional employment. Both now work for the City of Kansas City, Missouri. Their beautiful daughter Ana was born in the U.S. and has never been to Baku.

As far as food goes, Igor makes the best Turkish-style coffee in Kansas City, period. He also makes some of the best kebabs. Karina cooks a variety of fantastic dishes customary in Azerbaijan and Armenia. I especially like her eggplant recipe, which she cooked for this book.

Grandma Opal's Cornbread

By Rebekah Moses and Pablo Marin

1/2 cup canola oil

2 cups self-rising corn meal mix

1-2 tbsp sugar
(or more, depending on how sweet you like it)

3 tbsp all-purpose flour

1/2 cup milk

1 egg

OPTIONAL
whole kernel corn
bacon
diced jalapeños

Preheat oven to 425° F. Pour oil in a 10″ cast iron skillet or any oven-safe pan and place in oven for a few minutes to heat. Mix cornmeal, flour and sugar. Add milk and egg and mix well. For a more interesting taste, you may add whole kernel corn, bacon or diced jalapeños to your batter.

Add a small amount of hot oil into the batter, mix well. Pour the batter into the skillet with oil and bake for 20 minutes or until a toothpick comes out clean. Flip cornbread to other side and bake for an additional 5 minutes, or until top is browned.

Serve piping hot or cooled. Top with butter, molasses, jam, honey or whatever your heart desires. Also delicious when dunked in coffee, milk or buttermilk.

REBEKAH'S ODE TO PABLITO

Colombian Independence Day Party 2002, Kansas City, Kansas,USA. That's where I met my Pablo. He was wearing a "zapote"- (tangerine) colored shirt. I was wearing the tightest, shortest thing in my closet. He asked me to dance.
I thought he was the most boring Colombian salsero I had met.
He thought I was a Gringa who had no rhythm.
His eyes were shiny black. My walls came down. Six months later we got married.
I love Pablo because he thrives despite culture shock, English-only and xenophobic bigots
I love Pablo because he has taught me to listen; I am just a slow learner.
I love Pablo because he gives without expectations. He accepts people without judging.
I love Pablo because he inspires me to be a better person
and to be grateful for what I have: a cornucopia of opportunities which drive and entice the Pablos of the world to this country – in spite of all odds.
I love Pablo because he reminds me of my connection to others, be they Americans or Palestinian. He reminds me that what my country does abroad has consequences in my own backyard. Suffering cannot be exported indefinitely without a huge trade deficit.
I love Pablo because he cracks my back and budgets the money.
But most amazing of all, Pablo loves me. Even though I am a hag in the morning and I fold clothes horribly. Even though I need my own blanket in the bed at night. He loves me in spite of me. Thank God both of us are Salsa dancers.

~ by Rebekah Moses

Poori and Potato Masala

By Gayathri Ramaswamy and Ramaswamy Subramanyam

Poori

Mix wheat flour, salt and oil and knead well by occasionally adding water so that the dough becomes soft. Make the dough into smooth, round, even-sized balls of 2" diameter. Use a rolling pin to flatten the balls, one by one, make them round and flat of medium thickness. Deep fry the flattened pieces of dough in oil until the poori puffs up fully.

Potato Masala

Cook potatoes in pressure cooker or boil them in a pot. Peel the potatoes and mash them. Cut onions and chilies into long, thin slices.

Heat oil in a frying pan and add the seasonings. When the oil begins to splatter, add onions and chilies. Fry until they become light brown. Add tomatoes and fry for two more minutes. Add thick tamarind extract, salt, turmeric powder and 1/2 cup of water.

When ingredients start boiling, add mashed potatoes. Stir well and reduce flame. When the masala becomes thick, remove from heat and serve hot with poori.

Seasoning

Mix seasoning ingredients, serve with poori and potato masala.

We moved to *the United States from India due to Ramaswamy's job transfer. We enjoy our lives here as immigrants, experiencing the variety of culture and most of all, the different kinds of food. We enjoy the many opportunities provided by this country.*

We made Poori and Potato Masala, a dish that we enjoy eating for breakfast, or as a snack at any time of the day. The main ingredients, bread and potatoes, are common all over the world, making this dish versatile. Most importantly, this dish is a favorite in our house because our nine-year-old daughter loves it.

~ by Gayathri Ramaswamy

POORI

1 cup wheat flour

1/2 tbsp PLUS 1/2 tsp salt

3 tsp vegetable oil

1 cup vegetable oil *for frying*

POTATO MASALA

1/2 lb potatoes

3 large onions

6 green chilies

2 tomatoes *diced*

3 tbsp vegetable oil

1/2 tsp turmeric powder

1 tsp salt

a bit of thick tamarind extract

a pinch of turmeric powder

1/2 cup water

FOR SEASONING
mustard
black gram
bengal gram lentil
curry leaves

Italian Tomato Basil Salad

By Susan and Alex Masson

6 large ripe tomatoes *quartered*

1 medium onion
coarsely chopped

garlic salt *to taste*

dried oregano *to taste*

fresh basil *coarsely chopped
to taste*

4-6 tbsp extra virgin olive oil

4-6 tbsp red wine vinegar

6-8 oz Italian Parmesan cheese
freshly grated, rather coarsely

Layer tomatoes, onion and basil in a deep bowl, sprinkling each layer to taste with garlic salt and oregano. Make 2 to 3 layers.

Pour olive oil over tomatoes. Pour red wine vinegar over oil. Cover with a layer of Parmesan cheese. Seal the bowl with plastic wrap and refrigerate at least 2 to 6 hours. Serve in individual bowls with fresh Italian bread to soak up the juices.

I called Alex *Masson and asked him, "Could you come to my house on Saturday and cook for my cookbook?" He replied, "You might like it better if Susan does that since she is the gourmet cook in the family." So Susan came down and made the Italian Tomato Basil Salad, which looked just as beautiful as it tasted. She told me that Alex's mother, Tena Masson, passed*

on this family favorite recipe. The Masson family has been in flowering plant producing and wholesale business since 1910, and their products sell under the Sunflower Sue label. Years ago, Italian merchants shopped their greenhouses in the spring for flowers to sell on street corners. Tena Masson made friends with one of the customers who shared this recipe with her. Now, many years later, it is ours to enjoy.

Ham Rolls

By Sergei and Natalia Bautin

Mix shredded cheese, shredded carrot, chopped garlic and mayonnaise in a bowl. Put 1 tsp of cheese mixture in the middle of a ham slice. Make a small roll and insert a toothpick with a cherry tomato through the middle of the roll. Refrigerate for 20 to 45 minutes before serving.

25 toothpicks

25 cherry tomatoes

25 pieces of finely sliced ham

4 oz shredded cheese
Parmesan, Mozzarella or Swiss

4 oz shredded carrot

1/4 tsp garlic *minced*

2 tbsp mayonnaise

My husband Sergei *Bautin and I were both born in Russia. Sergei is a professional hockey player. He is very good at what he does. So good in fact, that he was invited to play for many prestigious hockey clubs throughout the world.*

Our traveling adventures started soon after we married in 1992, when we left for Canada. Two exciting years later, our son and dearest travel companion, Andrei, was born. Sergei also played for clubs in Sweden, Germany, Russia, Japan and right here in the United States, in Detroit and Kansas City, so all three of us traveled from country to country. Amidst all of this travel, I was fortunate to be able to balance taking care of my husband and son while graduating with a degree in Computer Science from Park University in Parkville, Missouri.

As you probably know, traveling has its advantages and disadvantages. Some of the advantages are meeting new people, making new friends and eating new delicious and exotic foods like the ones listed in this book. From my many travels, I have learned to cook easy, healthy recipes that bring color, different tastes and countless memories from all over the world to our table.

~ by Natalia Bautin

3 boiled eggs *chopped*

4 oz canned tuna in
spring water, *drained*

2 oz onion *chopped*

2 tbsp mayonnaise

10-15 toothpicks

20-30 baby carrots

1 head iceberg lettuce

Tuna Salad Rolls

By Sergei and Natalia Bautin

In a bowl, mix eggs, onions, tuna and mayonnaise. Separate lettuce leaves. Put 1-1/2 to 2 tbsp of tuna mixture in the center of each piece of lettuce, depending on the size of the leaf. Roll together. Secure tuna salad roll with a toothpick, with a carrot on either side.

See Sergei and Natalia's story and photo on page 26.

In Georgia, cooks often make *bazhi* (paste of walnuts, garlic, cilantro and spices) ahead of time to be on hand for many tasty dishes. They simply mix *bazhi* with vegetables, meat, chicken or fish - combinations are endless, and each has its unique taste. One of the most popular and easy dishes is bazhi with red or green beans, called *lobio*.

Lobio ~ Red Beans in Walnut Sauce

By Archil Mdivani

Make *bazhi* by grinding walnuts with garlic and cilantro. Add salt, pepper, ground coriander and vinegar. Sauté onion and add to *bazhi*. Add drained red beans. Mix well with a large spoon. Serve with chunks of tomatoes and crusty bread. In summer, try using about a pound and a half of green beans instead of red beans - just break them into smaller pieces and boil for 10 to 15 minutes. I hope you will like how it tastes.

3 (15 oz) cans of red beans

1 cup walnuts

1 bunch cilantro *chopped*

salt and pepper *to taste*

1 tbsp ground coriander

2 tbsp vinegar

5 cloves garlic

1 medium onion *finely chopped*

3 tbsp olive oil

EQUIPMENT
meat grinder or food processor

Archil Mdivani is *my dad. He was born in Sukhumi and raised in Tbilisi, Georgia. He went to school to study avionics in the Ukraine, and then lived in Turkmenistan, Uzbekistan and Russia. Dad worked for Aeroflot, the Soviet Union's biggest airline, for nearly 30 years. Dad reads all the time - he would rather read a book than go fishing. I inherited his reading habits, reading several books at the same time, and there are books all over my bedroom. And then there is the Internet - Dad reads Russian and Georgian newspapers on line and gives us the world news update during dinner. Dad has been great help in raising our family. Thanks to Dad, both of my children speak a second language, Russian, without having to learn it at school. Dad cooks Georgian dishes which are to die for. He tells us which Georgian wines would go well with them. He learned some of the best dishes from other places he has lived in: tomato and onion salad from Uzbekistan (page 44) and borsch from the Ukraine, which I often ask him to make, especially in the winter. Dad is not having an easy time adjusting to life in the U.S., but I am grateful that he is here.*

Beets in Walnut Sauce

3 (15 oz) cans of beets *drained*

1 cup walnuts

3 cloves garlic

salt

freshly ground pepper

1 tsp ground coriander

2 tbsp vinegar

1 bunch cilantro

By Archil Mdivani

Grind walnuts with garlic and cilantro using a food processor or a manual meet grinder, transfer into a larger bowl, add salt, pepper, ground coriander and vinegar. This mixture is called *bazhi*. Your kitchen at this point will either "reek of garlic" or will be "filled with magical flavors of the East," depending on where you come from and how adventurous of a gourmand you are. Grind drained beets and add them to *bazhi*. Mix well with a large spoon. This dish should be served with crusty bread for better enjoyment.

See Archil's story and photo on page 30.

Beets in walnut sauce, beans in walnut sauce, chicken in walnut sauce - this means it is a birthday or a holiday, and my dad is in the kitchen cooking. He will call me and say, "Taste it. Enough vinegar? Enough salt? Enough pepper?" I taste it, tell him I have to taste it again to give him a definite answer, and will taste until it is clear that I should leave the kitchen or there will be nothing left for our guests. Make sure to decorate this dish nicely and tell your family and friends how tasty it is. Otherwise, it sounds too strange and they may try to avoid it. Once they try it, most will be hooked!

Leon Versfeld is *from Pretoria, South Africa. He speaks Afrikaans, Dutch, a little Sotho and Zulu, and flawless English, which is especially useful in Kansas City, because Leon is a lawyer. Before coming to the U.S., Leon practiced law in South Africa as an Advocate, "a lawyer who tries cases." Unlike in the U.S., where one law degree and a law licence is all we need to go to court for our clients, in South Africa, an additional law degree is required to be an Advocate. But in the U.S., lawyers cannot practice with licenses from other countries. In most cases, they have to go through law school again to be eligible to sit for the bar exam. Leon's case is unique. He petitioned the Missouri Supreme Court to look into his education and experience and let him sit for the bar without repeating his legal education. The Court was impressed, and Leon sat for and passed the Missouri Bar exam with flying colors! The other side of Leon's story is meeting Heather Hunter, a flight attendant who used to live next door to him. Leon fell head-over-heels in love. He proposed to Heather on her birthday, and off they went to North Captiva island to be wed on a sunny beach! Their new baby daughter's name is Annike, which means 'gracious' in Afrikaans. A fearless lawyer and a tough rugby player, Leon shares an observation about his immigration experience, "A lot of people do not know what level of anxiousness and sense of not-belonging many immigrants undergo while their future hangs in the balance throughout the tedious immigration process."*

Africa in a Puff Pastry

By Leon and Heather Versfeld

Whisk together marinade ingredients, place filets in a glass dish, pour marinade over filets, and marinate between 30 minutes and 2 hours. Preheat oven to 425° F.

Heat a skillet over medium heat. Add oil and butter, shallots, mushrooms and thyme. Sauté for 4 minutes, stirring occasionally. Season with salt and pepper and sauté for 2 more minutes. Add sherry and let liquid evaporate. Remove skillet from heat.

Remove meat from marinade and pat dry. Drizzle meat with remaining olive oil, season with salt and pepper. In a non-stick skillet over high heat, sear meat for 2 minutes on each side. Remove skillet from heat.

Spread the puff pastry sheet onto a lightly floured surface. Roll out pastry into a 12"x12" sheet and cut the dough into quarters with a sharp knife. Cover a cookie sheet with parchment paper and place the pastry dough onto it. Place one filet on each of the pastry quarters, and top with 1/4 of the mushroom mixture and 1 slice of Gouda cheese. Fold each corner to the top similar to an envelope.

Whisk egg and water for glaze. Brush the mix over the pastry pockets. Place the puff pastries into the oven at 425° F for 10 minutes or until golden. Once removed from the oven, let cool for 5 minutes before serving.

Photo provided by Leon and Heather Versfeld

3 tbsp extra virgin olive oil

1 tbsp unsalted butter

1 large shallot *coarsely chopped*

1/2 lb shiitake mushrooms *sliced, stems removed*

1-1/2 tbsp fresh thyme *finely chopped*

kosher salt *to taste*

fresh ground pepper *to taste*

3 tbsp dry sherry

4 filet mignon steaks

4 slices of quality Gouda cheese

1 sheet frozen puffed pastry *thawed*

1 egg

1 tbsp water

MARINADE

1/3 cup dry red wine *(We use Rooiberg KWV)*

1/3 cup Coca-Cola

1/4 cup extra virgin olive oil

3 tbsp honey

1/2 tsp kosher salt

1/4 tsp fresh ground pepper

Ukrainian Crab Meat Salad

16 oz crab meat or imitation crabmeat *cut into cubes*

6 boiled eggs *finely chopped*

14 oz can whole kernel sweet corn

6 scallions *thinly sliced*

4-5 tbsp mayonnaise

OPTIONAL
fresh parsley *chopped*
fresh fennel *chopped*

By Natalia Golovko Butler and Brian Butler

Put crabmeat, most of the chopped eggs, most of the parsley, fennel, and corn in a bowl. Add mayonnaise. Mix all ingredients together and then transfer into a pretty bowl. Decorate with remaining fresh parsley and eggs. Bon appétit! Easy and tasty!

Photo provided by Natalia Golovko Butler and Brian Butler

While swimming in the warm waters of the lake near my home in Missouri, I think about the beauty of doing laps and feeling absolutely free and strong. Then it hits me - I am not on vacation, I really live here now.

Brian and I met on an airplane in March of 2002. I was returning to my home in Kiev, Ukraine from a business trip. Brian was headed home from his father's funeral. We spoke for hours. Brian radiated kindness and amazed me with his openness. We parted at the airport with promises to keep in touch. As we continued to speak to each other through email, our feelings grew bit by bit for each other.

Brian proposed to me only two months after we had met! To be frank, the spectrum of feelings overwhelmed me. I was surprised, pleased, honored and scared. I realized that I had finally found "my" man. I took the proposal very seriously, but my responsibilities to my family and job in Kiev were also very important. Brian and I decided that I would visit him in the U.S. for a month to test our dedication to each other.

I met so many people in Brookfield, Missouri: Brian's family, friends, and members of the two churches that he serves. We toured Missouri's cities and even stayed at a church retreat center. It all felt so right that I decided to accept. We were going to marry each other!

To move to the U.S., we began filing a fiancee visa, which turned out to be heaps of paperwork. Thanks to the advice of our immigration lawyer, my daughter, Luda, also came the U.S. from Kiev State University before turning 21, the age-out deadline for children to be beneficiaries of fiancee petitions. After Luda and I moved to the U.S., Brian and I wed within a week at the local Presbyterian church. Luda was nearing 21 as we nervously waited months for a response from Immigration. We rejoiced when United States Citizenship and Immigration Services (USCIS) scheduled our interview.

When we arrived, the officer informed us that USCIS had lost our medical examination results. She also said my daughter was completely out of luck and would have to go back to the Ukraine. We were shocked. It turned out that the officer was new and did not yet know about a specific section of the law which applied to our case. Our lawyer worked hard on making sure the law was applied correctly and two weeks later she called us with great news; Luda and I were approved as permanent residents! Hurrah!! We could not believe our happiness. Little did we know that our immigration troubles were not over. Two years later, when we filed our Petition to Remove Conditions on Residence, which included Luda, Immigration forgot to approve Luda's case (again!). We were devastated. Our lawyer meticulously worked on correcting Immigration's error. The petition was approved, but we are still waiting for Luda's actual "green card."

~ by Natalia Golovko Butler

Tennessee Cabbage

By Sue Storm

Put butter into skillet on low to medium heat and let brown slightly, add cabbage and stir well.

Cover skillet tightly and simmer for 5 minutes. Stir and cook another 5 minutes.

Add salt, pepper and cream. Cover and simmer for 4 more minutes.

It is very important not to overcook the cabbage. This dish is ready when the cabbage is slightly tender.

3 tbsp butter

5 cups cabbage
shredded or sliced fairly thin

1/8 tsp pepper

1 tsp salt

1/2 cup cream, half and half or evaporated milk

How did I *come to be in this interesting cookbook? Though I am no gourmet chef, my family loves my cooking. My excursion into the world of immigration began when Melinda Lewis of El Centro crossed my path back in the summer of 2002. Melinda asked if I would introduce legislation for a Kansas Dream Act, a statute that would allow students, regardless of their immigration status, to attend our public colleges and universities at the in-state tuition rate. I am an educator by profession. Melinda's suggestion certainly made sense to me. And so we began ... with enthusiasm, energy and hope. Through this process, I had the privilege of visiting with Kansas high school students that are more likely to fulfill their dreams under this legislation. Their stories were heartwarming and encouraging. More and more of my colleagues came to realize that the Dream Act was the right thing to support, not only for these students, but for all of Kansas.*

Kansas HB 2145 easily passed the House early in the 2003 session. As events unfolded, legislative leadership, bowing to extreme outside pressure, often dashed our hopes for passage. The quick progress stalled, stopped, sputtered and started up again. With the help of visionary senators, the bill finally passed in spring of 2004. Now, many bright, hard-working and hopeful students have something working for them: a university education is within their reach.

Through the entire process, education committees were blessed to have the guidance and expertise of immigration lawyers who explained and re-explained the complexities of immigration law. As we learned more, we came to understand the true plight of young people due to long waits with Immigration and the red tape and inconsistencies that they and their families face as they try to become legal permanent residents and citizens.

~ by Sue Storm

Green Beans and Garlic

By Sue Storm

1-1/2 lbs fresh green beans
broken in half if beans are long

15-20 cloves of garlic

country ham *to taste, sliced into 1/4 inch cubes*

3-4 tbsp olive oil

water

Boil garlic for 8 to 10 minutes in a large kettle or pot. Remove garlic and set it aside.

Add beans to water and simmer for 6 to 8 minutes, until bright green.

Mash garlic cloves and sauté garlic in olive oil for one minute. Add ham and continue to sauté until cooked. Toss with beans. This sounds like a lot of garlic, but cooked in this way, the taste is sweet, not strong.

See Sue's story and photo on page 38.

Cucumbers & Onions With Fresh Dill

By Sue Storm

Place cucumber slices in a colander. Sprinkle with salt, then toss. Let the cucumbers stand for 15 minutes, stirring occasionally.

To make dressing, stir vinegar, dill, sugar and pepper in a large bowl until the sugar dissolves.

Drain cucumbers well and pat dry. Add to dressing and stir to blend. Add onions and stir again.

Place in a covered, sealed dish and refrigerate between 15 minutes and 2 hours. You may want to stir the contents occasionally so that all the vegetables get the dressing mixture. Sprinkle with dill. Serve cold. On the second day, the vegetables are not as crisp, but still quite tasty.

2 English hot house cucumbers (OR 1-1/2 lbs of any other cucumbers) *unpeeled and thinly sliced*

1 tbsp coarse kosher salt

1 Vidalia, Texas sweet or ten-fifteen onion *sliced into rings or chunks and separated*

1/2 cup distilled white vinegar

3 tbsp sugar

1/2 tsp freshly ground black pepper

fresh dill *chopped*

See Sue's story and photo on page 38.

5 hard-boiled eggs

1 (15 oz) can pink salmon

1 medium onion medium
finely diced

1/2 cup any shredded cheese

4 oz butter

1 (16-20 oz) jar mayonnaise

cilantro *for garnish*

Salmon Mimosa

By Vladimir and Yelena Logashov

First layer: Separate egg yolks from egg whites, grate egg whites, put in a bowl, cover with a couple of spoons of mayonnaise. *Second layer*: Mix half of the salmon with half of the diced onion. Spread atop the eggs, cover with mayonnaise. *Third layer*: Grate butter over salmon and onion. *Fourth layer*: Spread the remaining salmon onto butter, cover with mayonnaise. *Fifth layer*: Grated cheese over salmon, cover with mayonnaise. *Sixth layer*: Grate the egg yolks over cheese. Sprinkle with cilantro.

Photo provided by Vladimir and Yelena Logashov

Vladimir and Yelena *Logashov are from Moscow, Russia. Vladimir is a violin maker. He came to the U.S. on an H-1B visa to make violins at KC Strings, Inc. in Mission, KS. Gregory Sandomirsky, Associate Concertmaster of the Kansas City Symphony, says that Vladimir's violins are unique and they remind him of old Italian instruments in that they combine an easy way*

to play with a noble sound. Gregory says, "We are simply lucky that Vladimir chose to practice his craft right here in Kansas City." Meanwhile, afer making violins, violas, cellos and double basses all day, the "luthier" (that's what violin makers call their profession) comes home hungry. His wife Yelena has shared with me one of the dishes Vladimir likes, a layered salmon salad.

Uzbek Tomato and Onion Salad

By Stanislav Ioudenitch and Tatiana Kouznetsova

Mix tomatoes and onions in a bowl, adding salt and pepper. Chop cilantro very finely, and sprinkle the salad for taste and beauty. Let stand no longer than 5-10 minutes, then serve with Uzbek Pilaf.

See Uzbek Pilaf recipe and photo on page 49.

10 medium tomatoes *thinly sliced*

2 medium onions *thinly sliced*

salt and pepper *to taste*

10 stalks cilantro

Stanislav Ioudentich and *Tatiana Kouznetsova don't usually have much time for cooking. Usually, they play the piano - both are concert pianists and music professors. They also spend a lot of time working with their daughter, Maria, to develop her musical talent. She plays violin. I am convinced that nature decided to place yet another genius in this family, so watch out for this name if you are a classical music lover: Maria Kouznetsova!*

Called "one of the world's most brilliant and accomplished young virtuoso performers," Stanislav won the gold medal at the Van Cliburn International Piano Competition in 2002. For the past two years, it was easier to reach him in Shanghai, London or New York than in Kansas City. Recently though, he has been spending most of his time with his family and students, due in part to his increasing responsibilities as Park University's Artistic Director for the International Center for Music and the Youth Conservatory for Music.

Despite all of the above, I go to their house to enjoy great food. In Uzbekistan, where Stanislav and Tatiana were born and raised, making good pilaf is a matter of national pride. Stanislav has cooked it all over the world - most recently, during a picnic in the Italian Alps where he relaxed with his family after the European concert tour. How good is Stanislav's pilaf? Some say, as good as his music! Pilaf, however, is not complete without Tatiana's involvement. She makes the Uzbek Tomato and Onion Salad, which makes the whole experience simply unforgettable.

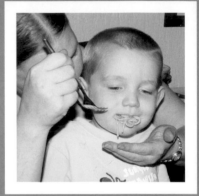

MAIN COURSE

PICTURED FROM TOP, LEFT TO RIGHT: *Moscow Newlyweds Fish; Mahadevan and Chithra Puliadi with their daughter; Washing basmati rice; Asado on the grill; Rita Witt; Mira Mdivani feeding her son Alexey; Stanislav Ioudenitch; Michael and Simran Nutter; Nancy Dobson checking on the Lancashire Hot Pot.*

This recipe is the Argentine version. The original tortilla de papas from Spain is spicier and includes onions. Leyla McMullen's mother, Esther Galmarini was the one who actually cooked it in my kitchen while the families looked on in anticipation. Tortilla de Papas was eaten fast, and both children and adults loved it.

Tortilla de Papas

By Leyla Galmarini McMullen and Jim McMullen

Heat oil in skillet. Use enough oil to cover the potatoes. Fry potatoes until cooked, but not browned. Remove cooked potatoes from oil and place on paper towel to absorb excess oil.

In a large bowl, beat eggs, while adding salt and parsley to taste. Then add both cheeses and cooked potatoes. Mix lightly. Coat a frying pan with enough oil to prevent food from sticking. Pour potato and egg mixture into pan and cook on low heat until the bottom is cooked, but not brown. You may need to use a spatula to prevent the bottom from sticking.

Place a large plate on top of pan and turn the pan upside down so potato mixture is on the plate. Then slide potato mixture back into pan, the uncooked side down. Cook this side until golden, not brown. You may have to push down with a fork to ensure that the egg part of the mixture is evenly spread. When the inside looks cooked, place a clean plate on top of the pan again to remove.

Photo provided by Leyla Galmarini McMullen and Jim McMullen

3 large potatoes *diced*

1 to 2 cups of vegetable oil

5 eggs

2 tbsp Parmesan cheese

1 tbsp shredded Cheddar cheese

salt *to taste*

parsley *optional*

We are Jim *and Leyla McMullen. We have four little kids (Ana, David, Daniel and Andrew), one puppy and two law degrees. We don't cook much, so this recipe is special! We ended up in this book after I met with Mira Mdivani to apply for an immigration lawyer position at The Mdivani Law Firm in July of 2004. One week later, my husband, my mother Esther, my four children and I were cooking for this book at her house, and tasting the other great recipes.*

I am originally from Argentina, so we decided to make tortilla de papas, a popular Argentinean side dish. My mom used to make it a lot when I was little. It goes well with asado meat (see Pastor Herlein's carne asado recipe on page 51). The first time I made tortilla for my kids, they did not want to try it because it did not look like a chicken nugget, a pizza, or a French fry. I told them it was a "potato pie." Any time you call something a "pie," your kids suddenly become more interested.

The red plate you see in the picture is a tradition we started in our home, one we copied from my husband's family. This is how the red plate works: One person in the family gets the red plate for dinner for being special. If it is your birthday, you automatically get the red plate. Another way to achieve red plate status is through doing good things, such as a goal at your soccer game; getting a good grade; helping mom unload the dishwasher; going in the potty (for this one you get the red plate all day!) The red plate gives the kids something to look forward to at dinner time. I hope you enjoy our tortilla de papas!

~ by Leyla Galmarini McMullen

Uzbek Pilaf

2 lbs rice

1 lb lamb

1-1/2 cup olive oil

1 lb carrots *peeled and cut into thin, 2-inch strips*

3-4 onions *sliced into 1/4-inch rings*

salt and pepper *to taste*

cumin *to taste*

coriander seeds *to taste*

By Stanislav Ioudenitch and Tatiana Kouznetsova

Thoroughly heat large, sturdy pot, then add oil and heat to a very high temperature.

Fry sliced onion in heated pot until they become a brownish-gold color.

Cut the lamb into pieces about the size of half of your palm. Put meat into pot to fry with onions until the meat develops a light crust on the outside.

Add carrots to pot with the meat and onions that are already frying. Stir occasionally.

When the carrots are half-done (test by poking them with a fork), fill the pot with water to just cover the contents (the meat and vegetables are now called *zirvak*). Add the pepper, cumin and coriander seeds.

When the zirvak and water begin boiling, add salt to the pot and reduce the heat to "low." Cook for 30 to 40 minutes on low heat.

Wash rice well in cold water and add to the pot after the *zirvak* has been cooking on low heat for 30 to 40 minutes. Do not stir rice in with the *zirvak*! Pour water to cover the *zirvak* and rice, with a little bit of excess water on top. Bring the pot to an even rolling boil.

When all of the water has evaporated, lower the heat to minimum. Gently form the rice into a mound in the pot with a flat, slotted spoon. Poke a few holes through the rice with a chopstick or other thin wooden stick. Cover the pot with a lid. Cook for about 20 to 30 minutes more, depending on the absorbency of the rice. Carefully stir the rice and zirvak together in the pot.

You are now ready to serve. Make sure to place rice onto the serving dish first, forming a big mound. Remove meat separately from the pot and cut into bite-size pieces. Cover the rice with the meat. Top the dish off with some chopped green onion or boiled eggs for extra flavor and color. Serve hot for best taste.

"Pri-yat-ne-va A-pe-ti-ta," Russian for "Bon Apetit!"

Serve with Tomato and Onion Salad. See recipe on page 44.

See Stanislav and Tatiana's story and photo on page 44.

Asado with Chimi Churri & Rice Salad

By Pastor Jorge Herlein and Ester Paccot

Asado
Prepare grill. Salt and pepper meat to taste. Put meat on grill with bone side down. Once ribs are cooked to desired temperature, remove from grill and brush with Chimi Churri Sauce (see recipe below). Serve Asado with rice salad and a tossed salad. Chimi Churri sauce may also be served over rice.

Rice Salad
Boil rice in water with salt until cooked. Rinse. Mix rice, onion and pepper with remaining ingredients.

Chimi Churri
Put all ingredients in a dressing jar. Close tightly and shake well.

ASADO

6 lbs beef ribs
cut Argentinian style -purchase ribs at a Latin meat market and ask for the Argentinian cut

RICE SALAD

2 cups uncooked rice

1 medium onion *diced*

1 green pepper *chopped*

1 tsp salt

1 tbsp vegetable oil

1 tbsp white vinegar

CHIMI CHURRI

(makes one quart)1 tsp salt

2 tbsp fresh parsley *finely chopped*

3 cloves garlic *finely minced*

1 cup vegetable oil

1 cup white vinegar

1/2 cup warm water

I saw Jorge *and Ester with their daughters, Wanda and Tatiana, at the Vision de Amor church several months ago. I visited with them on a non-church-related matter, and Ester invited me to the service, saying, "You should come, we have a party for Jesus here every Sunday!"*

Jorge Herlein leads the Vision de Amor mission as pastor at the Olathe Baptist Church. I asked Pastor Herlein to cook for my book. Pastor Herlein, Ester, Wanda and Tatiana arrived at my house after seven in the evening, tired after the service and ready to cook something special on the grill. Pastor Herlein explained that they had to go to this special butcher who knew how to cut meat for Asado, Argentine style, making them even later than they had planned.

After cooking and eating delicacies from all over the world all day, we were all tired and stuffed full of food. When Pastor Herlein brought the steaming Asado meat from the outside grill, my dad said, "There is no way I can eat anything else; my stomach will burst if I do" (rough translation from Russian). But then, my dad tried a piece. He then put another one on his plate.

He then came back for more, by which time everyone was eating Asado with the Chimi Churri sauce and the Rice Salad. "This is the best meat I have ever eaten," said Vesna Jokic, who usually does not even eat meat.

Ester was beaming. She said, "This is exactly how it is in Argentina!" She and Jorge brought happiness from their home and shared it with their new neighbors.

4 duck leg portions thighs attached, excess fat trimmed and reserved (about 2 pounds)

1-1/2 tbsp PLUS
1/8 tsp sea salt

1/2 tsp black pepper
freshly ground

12 garlic cloves (with skin)

4 bay leaves

5 sprigs fresh thyme

1-1/2 teaspoons black

peppercorns

1/2 tsp table salt

4 cups olive oil

Duck Confit

By Laurent and Kathy Denis

Place two duck legs on a glass or plastic plate with skin side down. Sprinkle with 1-1/2 tbsp of the sea salt and black pepper. Lay the garlic cloves, bay leaves, and sprigs of thyme on each of the 2 leg portions. Put the other two legs on top of the legs in the dish, skin side up. Put the reserved fat from the duck in the bottom of the container, with duck legs. Add remaining 1/8 tsp sea salt. Cover and refrigerate for 12 hours.

Preheat the oven to 200° F.

Remove the duck from the refrigerator. Remove garlic, bay leaves, thyme and duck fat from the duck and set aside. Rinse and dry the duck pieces. Put reserved garlic, bay leaves, thyme and duck fat in the bottom of an enameled cast-iron pot. Add peppercorns and remaining salt on top. Place the duck pieces, skin side down in the pot. Cover and bake for 12 to 14 hours at 200° F, or until meat becomes tender enough to pull away from the bone.

Remove duck from fat, strain fat and keep it aside. Serve the entire leg, or remove meat from the bones. If you are not serving it right away, add some strained fat to cover the meat.

Duck Confit can be stored in the refrigerator for up to one month. The excess fat can be stored in an airtight container in the refrigerator and used like butter for cooking. In France, we often use this fat to fry potatoes, cook green beans and sauté vegetables.

Photo provided by Laurent and Kathy Denis

Pommes Sardalaises ~ Sautéed Potatoes

By *Laurent and Kathy Denis*

POMMES SARDALAISE: Sautéed potatoes with garlic and parsley, Sarlat style.

Cut the potatoes into thin slices. Heat the fat in a wide frying pan or skillet, add the potatoes and fry for approximately 15 minutes. Turn potatoes over carefully, browning each side.

Once potatoes are browned, add salt, pepper, chopped garlic and parsley and pour in the rest of the fat. Fry for 15-20 more minutes, continuing to turn over carefully. Serve immediately.

Pictured left with Duck Confit.

4 lbs potatoes
peeled, rinsed and dried

1/2 cup goose fat
(may be substituted with duck fat or vegetable oil)

6 cloves garlic
peeled and chopped

salt and pepper *to taste*

Kathy and Laurent *met in Bordeaux, France. Kathy grew up in Kansas City, took French classes at the University of Kansas in Lawrence, and went to France on a scholarship to study business. Before long, she met Laurent, succumbed to his charms, and decided to stay with him in France.*

Together they explored the beautiful Bordeaux region, visiting vineyards, tasting Bordeaux wine, and enjoying some of the greatest food in the world. In 1995, Kathy and Laurent married in a storybook ceremony in an 11th-century church in the Dordogne valley. After their wedding, they decided to try life in the New World and came to settle in Kansas City. Their love for wine, food, and cooking led them to publish "The Kansas City Restaurant Guide," which has become simply the best source of information about where to eat well in Kansas City.

Duck Confit and Pommes Sarladaises recipes come directly from the Dorgogne region of France, where Laurent and Kathy spent a lot of time and which they remember with special fondness.

Chicken Biryani

By Chithra and Mahadevan Puliadi

Mix garam masala powder, coriander, turmeric, and 1 tsp of salt with the yogurt. Add chicken pieces and mix. Set the chicken aside for 1 hour.

Heat oil in a Dutch oven or pressure cooker. Add garlic, cardamon, bay leaves and cinnamon. Add onions and sauté until they become translucent. Add ginger and garlic paste and continue to sauté for several minutes. Add tomato and sauté until it becomes soft and mash it together. Add chicken pieces from step 1, all of the yogurt, and continue to sauté until the chicken is half-cooked.

Wash the rice well and drain it of all water. Add the rice to the chicken and blend the contents well. Pour the water over the rice and add the rest of the salt. Mix well. Close the lid and wait for the pressure to build. Cook on low heat for another 5 minutes once the pot reaches maximum pressure. Wait for 15 to 20 minutes for the pot to release all of its pressure. Open the cooker and garnish contents with cilantro to serve.

2 cups Basmati rice

1 lb chicken *boiled and sliced into small pieces*

1-1/2 medium onions *finely chopped*

1 tbsp ginger *minced*

1 tbsp garlic paste

1 tsp red chili powder

1 tbsp coriander powder

5 garlic cloves

5 pieces cardamon

2 bay leaves

1 cinnamon stick *1-inch long*

1 tsp turmeric powder

3/4 cup plain yogurt

3/4 tsp garam masala powder

6 tsp vegetable oil

2 tsp salt

1/2 cup tomato *chopped*

3-1/2 cups water

2 tbsp fresh cilantro *chopped*

EQUIPMENT

Dutch oven or pressure cooker

My husband, Mahadevan *Puliadi and I were born and raised in a city named Madurai in the southern part of India. Maha worked in Bombay, India, where we married and lived for several years. Bombay, one of the biggest cosmopolitan cities in India, bustles with people and business just like New York. Our two daughters were born while we were living in Bombay.*

In 1997, we all moved to Kansas when Maha received a job opportunity that appealed to him.

The company for which he worked decided to file for his green card to allow Maha and our family to remain in this country for as long as we chose to stay. It has not been easy - the wait and the uncertainty of it all, but we hope all will go well in the end. We wanted to participate in this cookbook and are very pleased to share our family's recipe with others. We hope that everyone will enjoy this exquisite Indian dish.

~ by Chithra Puliadi

Quick and Easy Garlic Shrimp Pasta

By Rita Witt

1 lb spaghetti

I lb frozen shrimp
cooked, peeled and deveined

1 cup olive oil *(extra virgin, cold pressed for more flavor)*

1 tsp Italian seasoning

1 tsp celery salt

4 cloves garlic *minced*

3 bay leaves

grated Parmesan cheese *to taste*

salt and pepper *to taste*

oregano *to taste*

GARNISH
lemon slices
fresh basil

Put 8 quarts of lightly salted water into a tall pot, cover and place on high flame to boil. Defrost shrimp in cold water and drain. Once the spaghetti water has begun to boil, begin to heat olive oil in a large skillet over low flame. Add Italian seasoning, garlic, celery salt and bay leaves to the skillet. I like to use an old iron skillet because it seems to work best for even heat.

When the spaghetti water reaches a rolling boil, stand spaghetti on end in the pot, twist slightly and drop in the boiling water. Stir for one minute, until strands are separated. Boil until spaghetti is al dente: firm but not crunchy. Drain it in a collander, but do not rinse. Meanwhile, once the seasoned oil is hot on the skillet, stir in the shrimp and increase heat to medium. Continue to stir for 3-4 minutes until the shrimp begins to curl, but do not overcook it.

Once the shrimp is done, spoon it out of the mixture and place into a bowl. Remove the bay leaves. Reduce the heat under the seasoned oil to very low.

Pour the drained spaghetti into the oil in the skillet and stir to absorb flavors. Stir in the shrimp and turn off the flame. Serve pasta topped with a generous amount of Parmesan cheese, and sprinkle with salt, pepper and oregano to taste. Garnish with lemon slices and/or fresh basil.

As the second *oldest of 11 children, I grew up on a small farm outside of Pierce City, a small town in the southwest corner of Missouri. At eighteen, I left home armed with courage, faith, determination and a lot of practical knowledge, all gifts from my parents, and entered a Franciscan Convent. After ten years of studying, teaching in small rural schools in Missouri and working with college kids, divine coincidences intervened. I left with two other nuns to begin a mission in Cruzeiro Do Sul, Acre, in the heart of the Amazon Rainforest of Brazil. I lived in Brazil for 15 years.*

During my time in Brazil, I did a little bit of everything. I first helped adults to complete grade school, then high school, then teacher training. I became a mid-wife and worked in health care, traveling around in boats and small canoes to the far reaches of the great Amazon River. I started and coordinated a Center for the Defense of Human Rights and worked within the

juvenile/family court system with abused and abandoned children. For someone from Pierce City, Missouri, this was an incredible adventure into all the wonders of another culture, another language, another way of perceiving life.

My experiences with the immigration process began with my own immigration as I plowed through getting permanent residency in Brazil. I know very well the importance of

....continued on page 83

This dish is very tasty and impressive. It amazes spouses and dinner guests and looks like something you have spent hours cooking. However, it is so easy to make that really good cooks in Moscow never cook it because everyone knows that even newlyweds, who are not supposed to know how to cook well, can dish it out with no effort.

Moscow Newlyweds Fish

By Mira Mdivani

Preheat oven to 400º F. Place fish in a 9"x13" deep baking pan. Sprinkle with salt and pepper.

Spread sliced onions over the fish to completely cover it. Then spread the shredded cheese over the onions. Again, cover completely. Next, spread on the mayonnaise. The most effective method I know is to take heaping tablespoons of mayonnaise and throw mayonnaise onto the cheese in different places. Then use the spoon to smother it over the cheese, so that all of the cheese is covered in mayonnaise. Then, place in oven for about 20 minutes. Reduce heat to 375º F and bake another 15 to 20 minutes or until the dish looks golden. The result will be, ahh...

Note: Instead of fish, you can cook beef or pork in the same manner with the same impressive result.

2-3 lbs white fish filets *cut into pieces of 2-3 inches each*

3 large onions *halved and sliced*

2-3 cups shredded cheddar cheese

9-10 heaping tbsp mayonnaise

Salt and pepper *to taste*

See Mira's story and photo on page 6.

Lancashire Hot Pot

6 lamb chops

olive oil *for braising*

2 large carrots *peeled and diced*

1 large onion *diced*

2 lbs potatoes *sliced*

1/2 pint of stock
(vegetable or beef)

2 tbsp melted butter

salt and pepper *to taste*

OPTIONAL

mint *finely chopped*

2-3 lamb kidneys

By Steven and Nancy Dobson

Preheat oven to 300° F.

Braise the chops in a frying pan with oil. Transfer to a ceramic pot. Place lamb kidneys (optional) around the chops. Add carrots, onions and mint. Top with potatoes. Brush melted butter over potatoes. Add stock. Salt and pepper to taste.

Cover pot and cook in a medium oven at 300° F for 2-1/2 to 3 hours. Uncover the pot, increase temperature to 375° F for 20 minutes. This will brown the potatoes. It's ready to serve.

Three years of marriage have provided Steven and I with endless wedded bliss. Working on Steven's U.S. permanent residency, however, has been an entirely different story. I am from Missouri. Steven is from Lancashire, England. We met on the Internet, of all places. Both Steve and I are U.S. Civil War enthusiasts. I have to admit that Steven might know more about the States than I do. We both participated in cancer support groups, each having lost a loved one to cancer. We spent time visiting each other and traveling, and before long, we were on our way to get married. Steven's immigration to the U.S. began with applying for a fiance visa. I searched for legal counsel first. The immigration process takes a lot of time, paperwork, patience and money. It barges in on your privacy, and it tries your stamina, so you need the expertise and support of a professional. We ran into unexpected complications right way. Scotland Yard lost Steven's background check, and Steven's U.S. consular processing was severely delayed.

Steven arrived in America on Valentine's Day, 2002 (what a romantic!) Our wedding was fun and heartwarming. I was diagnosed with multiple sclerosis six weeks later. Steven has been responsible for the two of us ever since, working, taking care of me and improving our farm, but his green card kept being delayed. Immigration kept saying it was the "background checks." Two years after Steve's move, when his father became critically ill, Immigration still had not approved Steven's green card. Steven had to apply for permission to travel. Our lawyer prepared the application immediately, but dealing with Immigration was a hellish ordeal. Instead of sympathy and help, Immigration officers treated us harshly, doubting the authenticity of e-mails from

England, and refusing to issue the permission until our lawyer took the matter up with a supervisory officer. A simple matter that should have been resolved without delay took days of anguish before the document was issued. Later, after a long wait, Steven finally received his green card. We now live without fear, cherishing our hopes and dreams, and looking forward to 2007, when Steven can become a U.S. Citizen.

~by Nancy Lee Dobson

Dad finished cooking Chicken Tabaka, set it on the kitchen table, took off his apron, and went to the bathroom. When he came back a couple of minutes later, he said, "OK, let me see how it turned out." Three of my friends (no names here...) stood in my kitchen with their oily hands up, mouths full, and a guilty look in their eyes. They had finished it before dad had a chance to taste his own creation! They were grudgingly forgiven: after all, it was a really small Cornish hen and I think dad was kind of proud of how quickly it had been devoured.

Chicken Tabaka

By Archil Mdivani

Rinse chicken and cut along the breast. Press or pound the chicken to make it as flat as possible. Mix minced garlic with sour cream. Add salt, pepper, coriander, cilantro and basil. Mix well. Massage sour cream into the chicken, making sure it is spread evenly on both sides of the chicken. Set aside for 15 to 20 minutes.

Pour olive oil into a large iron skillet. When the oil is hot, place chicken in skillet with the inside part of the chicken facing down. Place a plate on top of chicken, then add skillet weights (or something else that weighs at least 4 to 6 lbs). Cook on high for 15 to 20 minutes. Flip chicken and cook on high to medium heat for another 15 minutes. Chicken must be crispy crisp! Garnish with cilantro.

Wash hands properly, close your eyes and eat with your fingers.

1 small young chicken or Cornish game hen

1 garlic bulb
peeled, crushed and minced

1/2 cup of sour cream

1/2 tsp salt

a pinch of black pepper

1/2 tsp dry coriander

1/2 tsp dry basil

1/2 tsp dry cilantro

1/2 cup olive oil

See Archil's story and photo on page 30.

Eschabeche de Pollo

By *Ninfa Indacochea-Redmond*

2 red onions *quartered*

2 red onions *finely diced*

3 cups red wine vinegar

8 chicken thighs, 8 drumsticks

3 hard boiled eggs *sliced*

10 Greek/Kalamata olives

10 Spanish olives

3 sweet potatoes
boiled and sliced 1-inch thick

3 ears of corn on the cob
boiled and cut into thirds

3 tbsp olive oil

salt and pepper *to taste*

Cayenne pepper or Hot Paprika
to taste

1 medium tomato *diced*

2 stalks of celery *finely chopped*

1 red bell pepper *chopped*

1 orange bell pepper *chopped*

1 green red pepper *chopped*

Boston lettuce

Cayenne pepper in this recipe replaces a Peruvian spice called "aji" which is difficult to get here in the U.S. Ninfa usually cooks this recipe as a meal for four people, but she says it may be served as an appetizer, too.

Boil the quartered onions for 2 to 3 minutes. Drain, cool and place onions in a bowl containing red wine vinegar. Soak for several hours.

Pan-fry chicken in olive oil on each side until cooked. Pat dry with paper towel.

To prepare the *ahogado* spicy sauce, sauté the diced onion in olive oil until browned. Add chopped celery and diced tomatoes and continue to sauté for a few minutes. Add salt, pepper and cayenne pepper or hot paprika to taste.

Spread the *ahogado* thinly across a plate. Add a chicken thigh and a drumstick. Cover chicken with onions soaked in red wine vinegar. Place lettuce around edges of plate. Place corn and sweet potatoes on the side. Top with sliced eggs, sautéed bell peppers and olives.

Ninfa Indacochea-Redmond *is kind and intellectual, drives a yellow convertible, speaks in a very low sexy voice, wears outrageous dark glasses, fancy shoes, speaks Spanish, Italian, French, Portuguese and English, and loves music and the arts. In addition, she is a pharmacologist-toxicologist with a PhD from the Universite de Montreal, a mother of two children, Margarita and Allen, and a grandmother of two beautiful granddaughters, Ariel Nicole and Talia Rose.*

Ninfa was born and raised in Peru, then moved to Canada. Later, she was invited to come to the U.S. because of her unique scientific expertise, and to my delight, she settled right here in Kansas City. Ninfa thinks she is retired.

That, of course, is an exaggeration. Instead of enjoying her retirement quietly, she has started

a second career as a freelance interpreter and language teacher. She is known to generously donate lessons of Spanish, Italian and French to her curious friends and their children. I do not know how she found time to come to my house to cook for the book, but she did - so here comes escabeche de pollo, a colorful Peruvian dish. Ninfa beautifully arranged the escabeche on a family heirloom, porcelain dishes brought by her father from Japan to Peru more than half a century ago.

Dennis makes entertaining in our house easy: he is the marinate-and-grill master. He grills any meat or chicken or fish he can gets his hands on, serves it on beautiful platters, and our guests love it every time. My role is to give him beautiful platters and to make space on the dinner table when the food is ready. No summer cookout is any good without barbeque for a native Kansas Citian: Lamb Kebab occupies a similar place in my husband's heart, so here it comes!

Lamb Kebab

By Dennis Ayzin

Cover the bottom of large pot or bowl with onions. Place meat densely on top of onions and sprinkle with salt, red and black pepper, and garlic. Create another onion layer completely covering the meat. Continue to layer meat with spices and onions, making sure that onion is the topmost layer.

Mix vinegar, lemon juice and water. Pour to cover meat and onions. If it does not, make more of the marinade in the following proportions: 2/5 lemon juice, 2/5 water, and 1/5 vinegar. Leave the meat to marinate for 6 to 12 hours. Make sure that the grill is blazing hot before cooking meat. Slide the meat onto the skewers. Cook on the grill very close to the flame, turning for even access to the heat. The meat cooks quickly and will be ready when it has browned. Lightly heat the serving plate. Serve the meat hot, on skewers for dramatic presentation. Sprinkle with chopped cilantro.

2 lbs lamb,
cut into 2-inch chunks

3 large onions
halved and thinly sliced

1/2 cup vinegar
(or white wine)

1 cup lemon juice

1 cup water

crushed red pepper *to taste*

10 cloves garlic *crushed*

salt and pepper *to taste*

1/2 bunch fresh cilantro
chopped

EQUIPMENT

flat skewers

Dennis Ayzin happens *to be my husband. I often mentally pinch myself: this gorgeous, smart, funny, kind guy is my husband? But this is a cookbook, not a love letter, so suffice it to say that he is a great father to our children and I am happy that I will be growing old by his side (I do not know if he is 100% happy, because I am often whiny and grouchy, which tends to get worse with age, they say). Back to the cookbook. We are a family with two small business owners: I am in charge of The Mdivani Law Firm, and Dennis has TranslationPerfect.com, an interpreting and translations company. His background is in computers, so on top of everything, he is a geek. Dennis says he is lazy, and in order to do less work, he writes software programs that help him manage interpreting and translation projects in dozens of languages. Jokes aside, however, it is common knowledge that small business owners do not have regular business hours. So who takes care of food? In our house, men (my husband and my dad) rule during the week and I mostly take charge on weekends. Dad spends hours making elaborate dishes, Dennis, on the other hand, will not cook anything that takes more that*

ten minutes of his time. But make no mistake: Dennis loves to eat, and he is a gourmet cook. Some of my favorites are grilled tuna or pan-fried cod, which comes out golden and melts in your mouth, cooked by Dennis in under the prerequisite ten or so minutes. Dennis is also the reason why we always eat a big green salad with every meal, very simple except for the dressing, which he whisks together effortlessly from secret ingredients.

Grilled Bratwurst

By Tien Bui

bratwurst

hotdog buns

ketchup

mustard

relish

onion *finely chopped*

EQUIPMENT
grill
charcoal
lighter fluid

Soak charcoal with lighter fluid and light. Wait until grill has heated properly and charcoal is hot. When ready, place bratwurst on grill. Rotate them periodically to make sure all sides cook evenly. Lightly toast buns on grill. Put bratwurst in buns when ready. Top with ketchup, mustard, relish and onions to taste.

Tien came to *the United States from Vietnam when he was two. While I was working on his case, I had the pleasure of meeting Tien's parents, Khai Quang and Duoc Bui. They had to give affidavits confirming his birth because Tien has no birth certificate. Tien's mother, Duoc, said that at the time of his birth, the ongoing Vietnam conflict was destroying everything in the country.*

When Duoc was in labor with Tien, his father, Khai, drove her to the clinic on his motorcycle. She sat sideways behind him and held on with her arms around him. She said, "The baby was coming so fast, I was afraid we would not make it." The clinic did not have a doctor anymore, but the remaining staff successfully delivered her baby. Fathers were not allowed into delivery room so Khai waited anxiously outside until the baby was born. Khai said, "They showed the baby to me later. He was sleeping, and I thought he had a big face for a baby." The family fled Vietnam soon after Tien's birth. Duoc recounts, "I just grabbed my children and nothing else, to save our lives."

Tien recently earned his degree in aeronautical engineering from The University of Missouri. He works for Boeing, building the next generation of America's airplanes. When he brought hot dogs and buns to my house to cook for this cookbook, I said, "Tien, that won't do. Why don't you cook something interesting? We are trying to put together a real cookbook here." Tien replied,

"Mira, this is what I love to eat and this is what I know how to cook." He grilled some great hot dogs, filling the backyard with smoke and Fourth of July flavors, luring everyone outside for the taste of a normal American moment: hot dogs, evening sun and all.*

* Tien filed his application to become a U.S. citizen in 2003. As of this writing, we still have not received a decision from USCIS regarding Tien's application.

Meat Pie

By Svetlana and Grant Topchiev

Dough

Sift flour onto your cooking surface and make an indentation in the center of the flour.

Combine sour cream, eggs, baking soda, and vinegar and place into the center of the flour. Begin kneading the contents together from the outside in until the dough is no longer stuck together. You can fold it in with your hands several times, but do not pull apart.

Place the dough into a container and seal tightly to prevent dough from drying. Let the dough stand in a cold place, such as a refrigerator, for at least 40 minutes, or preferably more.

Filling

Boil pork, along with whole onion, carrot and celery stalk. Remove the meat from the stock and mince.

Heat oil in a frying pan. Add chopped onions and fry to a golden-brown color. Add minced meat and simmer for 10 to 15 minutes, adding enough water to just cover the meat. Salt and pepper to taste.

Finely chop the hard-boiled eggs. Remove meat from heat and add chopped egg. Mix well.

Assembly

Heat oven to 360° F while assembling the pie.

Remove dough from its container and divide into two parts. Make sure that one part is slightly larger than the other. Spread and flatten the larger half of the dough on the cutting board with a rolling pin. Cover the layer of dough with the filling.

Roll out and flatten the second part of the dough. Cover the meat with this dough and seal the edges of the dough layers to completely enclose the filling.

Bake on a large baking sheet for 25 to 30 minutes at 360° F. Remove the pie from the oven when the entire crust is evenly golden.

See Svetlana and Grant's story and photo on page 83.

DOUGH

3 cups baking flour

8 oz sour cream

3 eggs

1/2 tbsp baking soda

1 tbsp distilled white vinegar

FILLING

1/2 lb pork

2 medium-sized onions
one whole, one finely chopped

1 carrot

1 celery stalk

2 eggs *hard-boiled*

Baked Macaroni and Cheese

6-1/2 cups cooked elbow macaroni

1 tbsp butter

4 cups milk

20 saltine crackers

5 cups shredded cheddar cheese

salt and pepper *to taste*

By Melinda Lewis

Melt the butter in a baking dish (souffle dish or 9-by-13-inch baking pan) and spread 2 to 3 cups of cooked macaroni over it. Top with a layer of shredded cheese and sprinkle with salt and pepper to taste. Top everything with 1/3 of the crushed crackers.

Add another layer of shredded cheese, salt, pepper and another 1/3 of the crushed crackers. Pour milk over both layers.

Finish with a shallow layer of macaroni and the rest of the crackers, ending with a generous layer of shredded cheese. Let the layers sit for 10 to 15 minutes so that the crackers can absorb the milk. Bake at 350° F until top is melted and crusty, about 30 to 40 minutes.

I was born *in Kansas City, Kansas, almost exactly in the middle of the United States, and had a very "middle America" experience growing up. My mom stayed home with us, in our house in the suburbs, and most of the people that we knew at school and at church were descendants of Europeans, generations ago, like me.*

I started studying Spanish mainly to give myself an advantage in the college preparation process. Traveling to Latin America opened my eyes to the poverty and desperation that had been only vague conceptions to me in my sheltered reality. I decided to use my social work training to not only serve the Latin American immigrants making their home in my country, but also to shed light on the injustices that create such hardships and trap so many who live outside of the comfort that is my life.

My current work at El Centro not only brings many new friends from around the world, and

creates a whole new world only miles from where I grew up, but has also forced me to look in the eyes of many victims of global economic, social and political realities, for whom the simple pleasures that defined my childhood, like arguing with my little sister over who got the most of the crusty top off my mom's macaroni and cheese, remain out of reach.

~ by Melinda Lewis

My mom got this recipe from a neighbor when we had a neighborhood potluck dinner after a play that my little sister and I performed in our backyard. We made a stage out of a clothesline and my mom's sheets and charged all of the neighbors 50 cents to see it. My dad ate almost all of the macaroni, so my mom asked for the recipe and started making it this way. We often ate it to warm up when it was cold outside. My mom sometimes made two servings so that we'd have enough for the whole family.

Beef and Guinness Stew

By George Vial

Cut meat into bite-size pieces. Brown in a heavy pot with olive oil. Add 1 pint of Guinness and braise at a low temperature for 2-1/2 to 3 hours until tender. Prepare onion, garlic and carrots and add to the pot with meat and continue to simmer. Add beef stock and simmer for one more hour.

Boil potatoes in slightly salted water until cooked. Drain potatoes but keep the water. Let potatoes stand for 20 minutes until firm again. Add potatoes to pot.

Add remaining 1/2 pint of Guinness and water left over from drained potatoes. Simmer for 10 minutes. Serve with warm soda bread and a pint of Guinness.

2 lbs stewing meat *lamb or beef*

2 lbs small new potatoes

3 large carrots *chopped*

2 medium yellow onions *thinly sliced*

3 cloves of garlic *minced*

1-1/2 pints of Guinness beer

1 pint of beef stock

2 tbsp olive oil

salt and pepper *to taste*

OPTIONAL

soda bread *can be found at any Irish import store*

George and I met *at a party – toward the end of the night when my inhibitions were completely out the window. I never imagined at that moment that we would one day be married. In fact, George did not come highly recommended (specifically by my best friend Beth). He was good looking and had a charming Irish accent we were sure he used to his every advantage. She had heard of his reputation and for the first few weeks, tried to deter me from seeing him every chance she got. Upon receiving this well-meaning and sound advice from a trusted friend, I ignored it.*

We went on one date a week for three or four weeks and I was sure George was sincere. I still wasn't looking for a serious relationship but he was nice and so funny. Okay, the jokes were a little lame (as they still are), but it's all in the telling, and George knows how to weave a story. There was a turning point in our relationship that took us from casually dating to becoming inseparable, and it was instant. I was very ill from a kidney infection – in a lot of pain with a high fever, and absolutely not looking my best. George came by with chicken noodle soup, medicine, and odds and ends that he thought would make me feel better. He spent the next few days being my nurse, just hanging out while I laid on the couch, tossing and turning in discomfort in a bath of sweat. So he wasn't so bad after all, kinda sweet actually, and Beth eventually saw that too.

George and I may have been cautious initially, but once we knew there was more to our relationship, it was a mad dash to the finish line. It seemed fast, how quickly we were moving, but when you know, you know. In the space of six months, maybe less, we moved in together and started talking about marriage. Since we were both in our final year of college, there was constant struggle – roommates, finances, life.

Six months after we met, George's mom passed away. It was a Sunday morning and

....continued on page 84

Pho ~ Vietnamese Beef Noodle Soup

By Ly Thi Duong and Linh Trieu

5 lbs beef knuckle, with meat

3 pounds beef oxtail

1 lbs flank steak

2 large onions, quartered

1 (3 oz) package pho soup seasoning - *contains star anise cinnamon stick and cloves*

1 teaspoon black peppercorns

1 4-inch piece fresh ginger *sliced*

1 tbsp sugar

1 tbsp salt

1 tbsp fish sauce

1 (14 oz) package dried flat, rice noodles

1/2 pound frozen beef sirloin *sliced paper thin*

1 lb cooked frozen meatballs *thawed*

1/2 lb tripe *boiled, optional*

cheese cloth

water

TOPPINGS

Sriracha hot sauce

Hoisin sauce

1 yellow onion *sliced paper thin*

1 bunch fresh cilantro

1/2 lb bean sprouts

1 bunch Thai basil

10 stalks saw leaves (culantro)

2 green onions *thinly sliced*

2 jalapeños *thinly sliced*

2 limes *quartered*

Sugar *optional*

NOTE: All ingredients can be found at your local Asian market.

Place beef knuckle, oxtail and flank steak in a tall stock pot. Season with salt, and cover with water. Bring to a boil and cook for about 20 minutes. Then, drain and rinse pot and bones. Return bones to pot, add about 6 quarts water (enough to cover bones) and bring to a boil. Lower heat to medium and simmer.

While broth is simmering, empty package of pho soup seasoning into a frying pan, add black peppercorns, quartered onions and sliced ginger. Sauté briefly (3 minutes or so) on high heat, just enough to release flavors. Tie all spices except onion in a piece of cheesecloth.

Skim fat and scum from soup and drop spice bag and onions into pot. Next, add sugar, salt and fish sauce. Periodically stir bones. In one hour, remove flank steak. Continue simmering uncovered over medium-low heat for at least 4 hours. Add more water if bones are not covered. When broth is done, skim fat, taste, and add salt as needed. Optional: cool completely (overnight if possible). When soup cools, fat is solid at the top and easier to remove than skimming.

Remove bones and spice bag from broth. Separate meat from beef knuckle, slice flank steak and set aside. Discard bones and spice bag.

Bring a large pot of water to a boil. Soak the rice noodles for about 20 minutes, then cook in boiling water until soft, about 5 minutes, drain. Do not overcook. Prepare tripe, meatballs and frozen beef sirloin. Set aside.

Prepare toppings: place fresh cilantro, saw leaves, Thai basil, beans sprouts, sliced jalapeño, onion and limes on a platter. Set table with hot sauce, hoisin and sugar.

To serve, place noodles into the bottom of a large bowl, and top with thinly sliced onion and raw beef sirloin, meatballs, tripe and beef knuckle meat (as much or as little as you can eat). Ladle boiling broth into the bowl, just covering everything.

Once the bowl is in front of you, add as many toppings as you like.

See Linh and George's story and photo on page 76.

The broth is what makes one bowl of pho stand out from the other. It should be clear and full of flavor. The fat must be skimmed off or else you end up with a very oily soup. Everyone adds different kinds of toppings to their soup. Some enjoy it "as is" with nothing added, but most people throw in a bit of everything – just tailor it to your tastes – spicy, sour, salty or sweet.

Pineapple Fried Rice

By Simran and Michael Nutter

Prepare and marinate shrimp.

Heat wok or a frying pan to medium heat and add 2 tbsp canola oil. When oil is hot, add half the diced onion and half the garlic. Sauté until the onion is transparent and garlic is golden brown and soft. Add shrimp and sauté until cooked. Remove mixture from wok and set aside.

Add 2 tbsp canola oil to the same wok. Sauté the remaining onion and garlic and sliced chili peppers until they soften in the wok. Add the cooked rice and stir until the rice is evenly coated with oil and spices. Add the fish sauce, soy sauce, white pepper and brown sugar. Stir until rice is evenly coated and heated. Stir in pineapples and cashews. Once thoroughly and evenly stirred, remove from heat. Garnish with green onions, Maraschino cherries and cilantro.

Simran and Michael *started to feel like "old friends reunited after a long time" on the night they met. Traveling halfway across the world, Simran, an exchange student studying at the University of North Carolina - Chapel Hill, met Michael at a friend's house in Ohio. Michael thought that Simran – a native of Singapore and resident of Australia that had somehow ended up at UNC – was fascinating. After many e-mails and phone calls, Simran came to visit Michael for several weeks after he moved to Kansas City. The trip changed their lives and eventually, they got married and Simran moved to Kansas City, too.*

Now, their baby boy Devin rules their lives, along with two huge and very friendly family dogs, Titus, a Doberman, and Zoë, a Rottweiler-Shepherd.

PINEAPPLE FRIED RICE

2 cups cooked Thai Jasmine rice *(refrigerate 3 to 4 hours or overnight)*

1/2 lb uncooked shrimp *peeled and deveined*

4 tbsp canola oil

1 small onion *finely diced*

5 cloves garlic *minced*

3 tbsp Thai fish sauce

2-1/2 tbsp soy sauce

1/8 tbsp white pepper

1/2 tsp brown sugar

2 cup pineapple *cubed*

1 cup roasted cashews

2 green onions *thinly-sliced diagonally*

2 sprigs cilantro *coarsely chopped*

a few Maraschino cherries

chili peppers to taste *thinly sliced*

SHRIMP MARINADE

1 tsp soy sauce

1/2 tsp white pepper

Refrigerate for 3-4 hours

2 lbs large uncooked shrimp
*peeled, de-veined and marinated
in 1/3 kebab sauce for 2 hours*

1/2 green bell pepper

1/2 red bell pepper

1/2 yellow bell pepper

1/2 orange bell pepper

1 medium Vidalia onion

1 small red onion

6 small red potatoes

1 cup cherry tomatoes

1/4 cup Maraschino cherries

1 cup pineapple chunks

Canned cooking spray

KEBAB SAUCE

2 cups pineapple juice

4-1/2 tbsp apple cider vinegar

4-1/2 tbsp brown sugar

2 tbsp corn starch

1/8 tsp crushed red pepper

1/8 tsp paprika

1/4 tsp dried chives

1 tsp ground ginger

1/2 tsp salt

1/4 tsp soy sauce

Shrimp Kebabs

By Simran and Michael Nutter

Sauce
Place all ingredients in a saucepan onto medium heat and mix with wire whisk. Stir frequently.

When mixture thickens (about 10 minutes of cooking), remove from heat. When cool, divide the sauce into thirds:

1. Shrimp Marinade
2. Grilling Glaze
3. Dipping Sauce

Shrimp Kebabs
Combine shrimp and 1/3 kebab sauce in a bowl, mix well, cover and place in refrigerator for approximately 2 hours. Cut all the peppers and onions into bite-sized chunks (approximately 1/2" to 1"). Set aside.

Cut potatoes into quarters and arrange separately on skewer. Assemble all remaining ingredients on skewer, including shrimp, as desired. Using a brush, generously spread grilling glaze on all kebabs.

Preheat grill on high to medium high. Apply cooking spray to grilling surface.

Place potatoes on grill, turning and covering with marinade every five minutes. Cook them for 10 minutes. Place remaining kebabs on the grill. Allow all kebabs to cook for approximately 3-5 minutes on each side. Cover with marinade after turning. Remove kebabs from grill and serve immediately over a bed of pineapple fried rice. Add dipping sauce, salt and pepper to taste.

See Shrimp Kebab photo on page 79.

See Simran and Michael's story and photo on page 80.

Entomadas

By Melissa and Carlos Castillo

Trim tops of tomatoes and chilies, roast them in frying pan on medium heat using no oil, until skin is blackened and flaky. Cut tomatoes into large chunks. Dice onions and mince garlic. Blend tomatoes and chiles in blender with chopped onion and garlic to make salsa.

Pour salsa from blender into a medium-sized sauce pan. Add salt and chicken broth. Heat on medium until thoroughly hot, but don't boil. Slowly stir in table cream to taste. The more cream, the thicker the sauce. Continue to stir until cream sauce is thoroughly heated, but don't boil. Meanwhile, heat enough vegetable oil in different frying pan to barely cover tortillas. Once hot, fry tortillas in oil until they are cooked, not crispy.

Next, using tongs, immerse cooked tortilla in pan containing cream sauce, then fold in half with tongs, trapping cream sauce inside. Top with grated cheese to serve.

Photo provided by Grant Wallace

3-4 large tomatoes

1/2 medium white onion
chopped

2-5 chiles, jalapeño or serrano

2 cloves garlic

1 tsp salt

2-3 tbsp chicken broth

8 oz Mexican table cream
or sour cream

6-inch corn tortillas
enough to match appetite

1/4 cup vegetable oil

semi-soft white cheese such as Queso Chihuahua, Queso Quesadilla, or Monterrey Jack

Carlos and I *met in Queretaro, Mexico when I was a foreign exchange student there. We fell in love, but I had to return to the United States to graduate from college. Leaving Carlos behind was the hardest thing that I ever did in my life. I eventually managed to save enough money to visit him again. After five months of separation, we were desperate to be together.*

....continued on page 84

having a good lawyer in your corner. I remember most my constant fear that I might not have correctly understood the directions in Portuguese.

When I began to work with abused and abandoned children through the courts in Cruzeiro do Sul, we at the mission helped with the adoption of 24 of these marvelous children to couples in Brazil, Europe and the United States. We were so totally involved! On more than one occasion, I assisted at birth, took the child straight to my room, cared for it for months, made the contacts with the courts and the future parents in the U.S., found the lawyer, nagged the judge, provided room and board to the adoptive parents and chauffeured them and the children back and forth over the dusty or muddy roads to the city to speed along the court process. My mission companions all did the same. I still have contact with some of these children and their parents today. Two of the beautiful little girls were under my legal guardianship for two years before we could finalize the adoptions.

Then, as swiftly as I came, I left, with the same divine coincidences changing my life's direction. I returned to the States and a "civilian" life, and started a commercial cleaning business to pay for my Master's degree in counseling, thinking I would return to work with women in Brazil. Instead, I interned at a local shelter for abused women, Hope House, and have been there ever since. I also re-encountered one of the college kids I had worked with 25 years earlier, Bill Capotosto (hence the pasta recipe) and finally got him to marry me in 2001! He is a

wonderful person, who is very supportive of my work with abused women and children and fits right in to my incredibly wonderful family.

Bill and I belong to a non-profit organization called Partners of the Americas. The state of Missouri is a partner of the state of Para in the Amazon forest of Brazil. Through Partners of the Americas, I have gone back to Brazil many times to work with women's groups to establish two domestic violence shelters there, train their staff and to help establish a hotline in a small city where women volunteer their time to keep it open 24 hours a day, seven days a week.

My passion for working for human rights, the opportunity to specialize in the area of domestic violence, my admiration for other cultures and divine coincidences brought Mira Mdivani into my life. In the United States, battered immigrant women, through the Violence Against Women Act, can gain legal status on their own (with the help of a great lawyer)! One day, Mira called wanting to know if I could do a domestic violence assessment for one of her clients, and a great working relationship began. I have done many assessments for Mira's clients, and have asked and gotten her help with Hope House clients that are battered immigrant women in need of legal representation. Now, she has put together this wonderful cookbook. I can't wait to see what she cooks up next.

~ by Rita Witt

Meat Pie & Lemon and Apricot Cake
by Svetlana and Grant Topchiev
....continued from page 72 and 93

I was born in Baku, *Azerbaijan in 1938. We used to have strong traditions in our family, and kitchen was treated in the most serious manner. My grandmothers and my mom were excellent cooks. Everyone admired their cakes and pastries. My mom, Eleonora, was especially creative at decorating her cakes and in how she set the table, with great taste. My husband Grant and I got married in 1965. We have*

two sons and two grandchildren. I would have never in my life thought we would be living in America, but here we are. I am happy to have my family here, safe and sound. I love cooking for them. I treat everyone who comes to the house to something tasty, and I love to entertain.

~ by Svetlana Topchiev

Beef and Guinness Stew & Pho ~ Vietnamese Beef Noodle Soup (continued from page 76)

we were just laying in bed, being lazy when the call came. Our bags were quickly packed as we rushed around thinking of what needed to be done before boarding our plane to begin the long journey to Ireland. My passport was just a few months old and completely blank – this was my first time leaving America since I arrived 25 years ago.

It was a somber trip filled with spurts of humor. Although we were there for the funeral, it was still my first time in Ireland and I was amazed by everything. The landscape, the houses, the colorful doors on every building, and the huge slices of bread on convenience store sandwiches. I loved it and could easily imagine living there forever.

But we had to come back home and finish school – the last six months were even tougher with much more stress and tension. And before we got a chance to breathe a sigh of relief at its completion, we had to tell our parents we were getting married. I was a nervous wreck. George is Irish and I'm Chinese. No big deal except no one in my family has ever married a non-Asian. On Mother's Day, with George's family over from Ireland to celebrate his graduation from Park University, and with my family and friends, we announced our engagement. Surprise! We're getting married next year, and surprised they were.

However, immigration matters arose, namely George's student visa expiring. We had a choice to extend his student visa or get married. It was simple – marriage it was, another unexpected surprise to our families. We had an informal and very intimate ceremony at our home, surrounded by friends and family who gave us their total support; they helped with everything from actually marrying us to cutting the cake. I was so nervous I laughed throughout the entire ceremony. Mira took care of the legal aspects and said, "Don't worry about anything. I will worry for you." We wisely did so.

We celebrated our one year anniversary with a Chinese wedding, a more formal, semi-traditional celebration. My family accepted George from the very beginning and I should have never worried. We continue to work through our cultural differences. We're in a place where hamburger and mince mean the same thing and we don't even realize it. We're Americans and we're immigrants. Sometimes it's a little unbalanced. Most of the time we never even think about it. But there are going to be a million funny stories to tell about how an Irishman and a Chinese girl fell in love in America and mostly lived happily ever after.

~ by Linh Trieu

Entomadas (continued from page 82)

I couldn't leave school to move to Mexico, so Carlos agreed to leave his family, his friends and his life behind to move to Kansas.

We had two weddings: one was a small civil ceremony in Kansas and the other, a spectacular church wedding in Mexico. My family met Carlos' family, which meant a lot to both of us, even though there were some language barriers. But it went well; even Carlos' 83-year-old grandpa managed to say a few phrases in English to welcome my parents. We visit Carlos' family at least once a year, usually at Christmas. His mom always cooks the most amazing food for us. Both Carlos and I look forward to her food all year long.

Two years after we got married, I decided to go to law school, which involved moving to a different city. Carlos once again left his friends, his job, and familiar surroundings behind in order to support me in my quest to become a lawyer. Carlos and I have been married for over five years now, but we still hate saying goodbye to each other when either of us has to travel without the other.

~ by Melissa Castillo

main course | 84

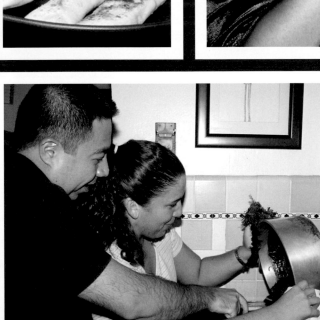

SWEETS

PICTURED FROM TOP, LEFT TO RIGHT: *Maria Iliakova and Dennis Ayzin; Tatiana and Wanda Herlein; preserved fruit for Halo Halo dessert drink; Turon frying in a wok; the Puliadi girls enjoying Fondant au Chocolat; Kathy Denis with the family dog; Laurent Denis with his daughter; Amber Hamilton and Abel Rivera making Mom's Fudge; Natalia Bautin and Mira Mdivani share a funny moment as they cook and clean.*

Oh! A taste of Brazil...any birthday party, baptism, wedding or friendly get-together is simply not complete without brigadeiros, a popular Brazilian dish. Simple, yet delicious, so rich, chocolatey and chewy, *brigadeiros* carry the sensuality and color of Brazilian culture and tradition.

Brigadeiros ~ Brazilian Bon Bons

By Monica Mingucci

Before you begin cooking the ingredients, lightly butter a plate. Place a saucepan over medium heat. Add condensed milk, cocoa and butter into the pan, stirring constantly to avoid charring until the mixture becomes thick (almost a caramel consistency). It will be ready when, if you run the spoon along the bottom of the pan the mixture separates for a second or two, so that you can clearly see the bottom of the pan.

As soon as the mixture is ready, pour it onto the buttered plate and spread evenly. Wait until the mix cools completely. You might choose to wait overnight or to refrigerate the mixture.

Next, pour the chocolate sprinkles on a plate. Wet or butter hands to scoop teaspoon amounts of the cooled mixture. Roll them into little balls (bonbons). If your hands get too sticky, wet them again. Run the bon bons on the chocolate sprinkles until bonbons are completely covered with them. Voila! Traditional Brazilian Bon Bons ready to serve!

---

1 can of sweetened condensed milk

2 heaping tbsp cocoa

1 tbsp butter, *as well as enough butter to grease a plate*

chocolate sprinkles

Yields 20 bons bons

I am originally *from Brazil. I have lived in the United States for 20 years. My husband is originally from Kansas City, and we felt it might be a good idea for him to come back home. Oh, the adventure of immigrating to a new country…*

We came to the U.S. in 1984 with three suitcases, a guitar, a two-year-old son, and $2,000. The economy was at its worst, and jobs were rare. So, obviously our beginning in the U.S. was rough, to say the least. Even though I spoke English fluently, had a college degree in Journalism and Mass Communication, worked as an English teacher and as an official interpreter for the Brazilian government, upon coming to the U.S. I had no profession. Since I desperately needed to work, I was lucky enough, and I mean it, to experience some of the traditional low-paying jobs available for the newly arrived in the U.S. I say that I was lucky because that experience reshaped my view of the world and gave me an opportunity to truly relate to newcomers to this land.

It was not until the nineties that things really began to change in my life. I returned to school and earned a Master's degree in Teaching English to Speakers of Other Languages (TESOL). Since I had extensive experience in the field, I was soon able to find more financially and intellectually rewarding jobs working with nonnative English speakers as a teacher, advisor and advocate.

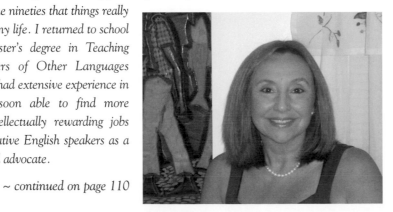

~ continued on page 110

Buttercream Cupcakes

By Sergio and Allyson Gonzalez

CUPCAKES

1-1/2 cups flour

1 tsp baking powder

1/4 tsp salt

1/2 cup sugar

3 eggs

2 tsp vanilla

1/2 cup milk

ICING

1 lb confectioner's sugar

1/4 lb butter, softened

1/8 tsp salt

1 tsp vanilla or other flavors and extracts

3-4 tbsp milk

sprinkles and food coloring *if desired*

Preheat oven to 350° F. Line 12 muffin tins with paper liners.

In a small bowl, mix flour, baking powder and salt. Set mixture aside.

With a mixer, beat butter until it becomes light and fluffy. Gradually add sugar, mixing on high speed until it becomes a pale yellow color. Reduce speed to medium, add eggs and vanilla slowly. Reduce speed to low. Add flour mixture and continue to mix until well blended, but do not over-mix.

Fill each tin 3/4 full of batter and bake for 20 minutes, until cakes spring back when pressed. Let the cupcakes cool before icing them.

To make icing, blend all of the icing ingredients together until they become a smooth mixture that can easily be spread onto the cupcakes. Add one or two drops of food coloring if desired. Sprinkle with your favorite sprinkles!

Sergio had grown *up baking in Mexico City. His father owned a bakery, and his father's father owned a bakery. As he got older, baking was all he knew. Sergio decided to break from the family tradition and become a lawyer. He finished law school, practiced law in Mexico for one year and decided that he must go back to his roots…baking! Sergio went to America to learn more about cooking and to become a prosperous pastry chef. He even took some of his cakes from Mexico City to California to showcase his talent. However, Immigration took all his cakes and sent him packing to Mexico, and maybe they ate those yummy cakes as soon as he was gone!*

But Sergio didn't give up. His sister was lived in Kansas City, and that's where he came next. He started working at the Marriott making beautiful pastries and wedding cakes that would impress the the most demanding chefs. This is where I come in!

I was studying at Kansas State University, in the field of hotel/restaurant management. My goal was to live in Oregon. I had dreams of Portland, near the Pacific Ocean and mountains

galore. I tried very hard to get an internship at the Marriott in Portland … everything was set up! I was going to live on a houseboat looking at the ocean every day. Then, the internship in Portland fell through. I was hopelessly sad. When they told me I could intern at the Overland Park Marriott, I wasn't very thrilled, but I took it. That's where I met Sergio.

….continued on page 110

Mocha Cake

By Sergio and Allyson Gonzalez

Coffee Syrup
Mix together very well, until a thin paste forms.

Mocha Cake
Preheat oven to 350° F. Melt the butter in a saucepan over low heat, then stir in the cocoa until blended. Set aside.

Beat the eggs with the sugar and vanilla until light, then stir in the cocoa mixture and coffee syrup. Sift the flours together twice. Sift them over the egg mixture a third time, folding each one in with a metal spoon.

Turn into a greased 8-inch cake pan and bake for 40 to 45 minutes. Take cake out of pan gently before cool and set on wire rack. Cool completely, preferably over night.

Simple Syrup
Boil all three ingredients until sugar is completely dissolved.

Oreo Cookie Crust
Preheat oven to 350° F. Mix all ingredients well, until moist.

Press into greased 8-inch cake pan and bake for 25-30 minutes. Let cool and take out of pan.

Mocha Buttercream Filling and Icing
Beat egg yolks in a bowl until they are pale and thick. Gently heat the sugar, water and coffee syrup in a heavy-based saucepan until dissolved.

Bring to a boil and boil until the syrup reaches the soft ball stage, 240° F. Gradually pour the syrup over the egg yolks, beating with a hand-held electric mixer until the mixutre is thickened and tepid.

Beat the softened butter gradually into the mixture. Mix in the melted chocolate.

Assembly
Cut cooled cake in three even layers. Drizzle each layer with simple syrup.

Place cookie crust on a platter. Place bottom layer of cake on top.

Spread 1/3 filling on layer. Place middle layer on top of bottom layer and spread 1/3 filling on top.

Place last layer on top and ice entire cake with remaining icing. Decorate with rosettes if desired.

See Allyson and Sergio's story and photo on page 89.

COFFEE SYRUP
- 1 cup instant coffee grounds
- 4 tbsp whiskey or rum

MOCHA CAKE
- 1/2 cup unsalted butter
- 1/2 cup cocoa powder *sifted*
- 2 eggs
- 1 cup sugar
- 1 tsp vanilla
- 1/2 cup all purpose flour
- 1/2 cup self-rising flour
- 2 tbsp coffee syrup

SIMPLE SYRUP
- 1 cup water
- 1 cup sugar
- 4 tbsp rum

OREO COOKIE CRUST
- 3-1/2 cups oreo cookie crumbs *or other chocolate cookie, mashed very fine*
- 3 tbsp cocoa powder
- 2 tbsp light brown sugar
- 6 tbsp butter

MOCHA BUTTERCREAM FILLING AND ICING
- 4 egg yolks
- 1/2 cup granulated sugar
- 1/2 cup water
- 1 cup unsalted butter *chopped*
- 3-1/2 oz bittersweet chocolate
- 2 tbsp coffee syrup

Lemon and Apricot Cake

By Svetlana and Grant Topchiev

DOUGH

2 sticks of unsalted butter

2 cups sugar

4 eggs, *separate yolks*

4 tbsp sour cream

1 tsp baking soda

1 tbsp vinegar

4-1/2 to 5 cups baking flour

FILLING

3-4 lemons

1/2 (6 oz) jar apricot jam

ASSEMBLY

1 cup walnuts *finely chopped*

Powdered sugar *to taste*

Blend butter in a blender until it becomes pale in color. Pour sugar into blended butter and blend well once more. Add the 4 egg yolks and sour cream to the butter and sugar.

Next, mix in the baking soda and vinegar. Combine with flour and the rest of the mixed ingredients. Knead dough until it becomes soft and pliable. Leave the dough in a cold place, such as a refrigerator, for at least 1 hour.

Preheat oven to 300° F. After removing dough from storage, divide into 3 equal parts. Roll out each third with a rolling pin into a flat, thin round. Bake each round on separate racks in the oven on baking sheets. Cook until golden brown in color.

Filling

Make before the rounds are done baking. It should be ready to use immediately when the rounds are cooked and while they are still hot.

Briefly scald lemons with boiling water and remove ends. Remove seeds from lemons. Place lemons in a blender and process finely.

Add apricot jam and mix well.

Assembly

Once rounds are finished baking, remove them and begin assembly immediately. *Caution: The baked rounds are very fragile: be careful when handling them, but make sure that you prepare the cake while the rounds are still hot.*

Cut each round in half lengthwise, making two thinner rounds out of each original round. Place a round onto the surface and cover with filling. Stack next round on top of filling, and continue until you have stacked all of the rounds and covered all of the cake with filling, including the sides. Top cake with the finely chopped nuts and powdered sugar. Decorate the cake with sliced lemon circles, cherries and mint leaves. Serve and enjoy!

See Svetlana and Grant's story on page 83.

Carski Kolac ~ Czar's Cake

By Vesna Jokic

Preheat oven to 400° F. Put all ingredients except chocolate and butter into a bowl and mix well. Place the mixture into a baking pan sheet of 11" x 13" and place into oven. Bake for one hour at 400° F. When done, remove from oven and let stand to cool.

While cake is cooling, melt butter over low heat in a sauce pan and add chocolate. Keep stirring until chocolate has completely melted into a smooth sauce.

Pour the chocolate over the cake and let stand until completely cooled. Sprinkle chopped walnuts over chocolate glaze. Cut into small squares to serve.

3 cups grated apples

1 cup whole wheat flour

2 eggs

2 cups ground walnuts

3-1/2 oz raisins

2 cups sugar

2 tsp baking powder

1-1/2 oz vegetable oil

1 grated lemon rind

1-1/2 oz rum

7 oz butter

7 oz baking chocolate

Vesna Jokic came *to the United States with her family from Bosnia via Germany. Both moves were triggered by her family's refugee status. Vesna thrived in the U.S., completing her education in modern languages on academic excellence scholarships. Now, Vesna is a U.S. citizen who is fluent in English, Spanish, German, Bosnian, Serbian and Croatian. She recently returned back to Bosnia to work as an interpreter for the United Nations. The recipe she cooked for this book is called the Carski Kolac, or the Czar's Cake, and you, too, will feel like a Czar or Czarina if it comes out well.*

KESARI

1 cup sooji powder
(or cream of wheat or semolina)

1-1/2 cups sugar

10 cashews *halved*

4 cardamon pieces

orange powder food coloring

ghee *as needed*

water *as needed*

BAJJI SNACK

1 cup chickpea flour
(Besan or Bengal gram)

1/4 cup rice flour

1 tsp chili powder

1/4 tsp asafoetida powder

1/4 tsp baking soda

4 cups vegetable oil

1 plantain

1 red onion

1 potato

salt *to taste*

water *as needed*

NOTE: Ingredients can be found in any Indian market.

Kesari PICTURED IN FRONT

By Felecia and Francis Kasi

Heat 1 tbsp of ghee in a pan on medium heat. Once it is hot, add sooji powder and fry until it becomes golden brown. Transfer mix to a bowl.

Add water to the empty pan and heat until it becomes hot, then add sugar. Slowly add food coloring and sooji to water. Stir until the mix become thick. Add water if the blend is too unwieldy.

Remove the pan from heat. Add more ghee and the crushed cardamon pieces to the mix. Stir contents well.

In a separate pan, melt 2 tbsp ghee. Add the cashews and fry until they become golden brown. Add the contents of this pan to the sooji and stir well. Place the combined contents into a serving bowl and serve warm.

Bajji Snack PICTURED IN BACKGROUND

By Felecia and Francis Kasi

Cut the potato and onion into thin rounds. Peel the plantain and cut it into thin long pieces.

In a large mixing bowl, combine the chickpea flour, rice flour, chili powder, asafoetida powder, baking soda and salt. Add enough water to make a smooth batter of dripping consistency. Heat the oil in a frying pan for deep-frying.

Dip each vegetable piece into the batter and fry until golden brown in color. You can serve this with various chutneys and other Indian sauces.

Francis is a *computer programmer from India who came to the U.S. on an H-1B visa and then fell in love and stayed! How do computer programmers date? On line! That's where Francis met Felecia - in an online chat room. Felecia, originally from Wilmer, Alabama, acquired a taste for Indian food while she was in India for their wedding. After years of experimenting with Indian recipes given to her by her mother-in-law and her Indian friends, she is now an expert in several South and North Indian dishes. Francis and Felecia have a two-year-old daughter, Jasmine, whom they plan to teach Indian culture and the language so that she knows her father's roots. At the same time, both parents agree that the future of Jasmine belongs in the United States, where Felecia and Francis want to see their grandchildren and great-grandchildren grow up.*

Mom's Fudge

By Abel Rivera and Amber Hamilton

Mix sugar, milk, cocoa and salt in bowl. Blend well.

In a heavy pan, cook the mixture at low to medium heat until the "soft ball stage."

The "soft ball stage:" fill a small bowl of water with room temperature water. Drop a spoon of the mixture into the bowl of water. If you can roll the little drop of mixture in the water to form a semi-firm ball with your fingers, you are ready to move on.

Fill the sink with cold water to create a water bath.

Turn the heat off under the pan and add butter, vanilla and peanut butter to the mix. Blend all of the contents well while they are still in the pan.

3 cups white sugar

1-1/2 cups milk

2/3 cup cocoa powder

3 shakes of salt

1/2 cup peanut butter

1 tbsp vanilla

1/2 stick butter

1/2 cup nuts *optional*

It's the middle *of a hot July day in my kitchen. Everyone in the house can hear Amber yelling at the top of her lungs, "Faster, faster, it's cooling down!" Amber and Abel are both holding on to a pot of hot fudge while trying to pour the fudge into a pan before it cools.*

When they are done, they kiss. I think, "Where is my video camera when I need it?" When I asked them to cook for this book, Amber and Abel wanted to know whether I was asking for a Mexican dish, since Abel is from Mexico. I replied, "No, this book is about all of us, both new immigrants and Americans in the fifth generation: cook what is dear to your heart."

They decided to cook an American dessert, which was handed down to them by Amber's mother. Says Amber, "My mom is the only one that can make it just right. Abel is allergic to chocolate but every time that she brings some fudge over, he just has to eat some. It won't be even 24 hours later that his skin begins to break out, but no matter, he still eats it every time." Share this fudge recipe and have some fun with your loved one!

Halo Halo

By Penny Porter Brosoto and Amiel Brosoto

jack fruit

coconut flakes

evaporated milk

tapioca pearl

coconut gel

sweet beans

purple yam (ube) spread
for topping

shaved ice

Parfait glasses
for a pretty presentation

NOTE: All ingredients can be found at any Asian market - preserved in jars.

Layer the fruits: Tapioca pearl, purple yam spread, coconut gel and sweet beans in the bottom of the glass. These ingredients should reach halfway up to the top of the glass. Next, fill the rest of the glass with shaved ice. Sprinkle coconut flakes on top and pour in 1/2 cup of evaporated milk. Top with purple yam (ube) spread.

Before drinking, stir all ingredients together so you can taste all the flavors. Now you have a cool summer drink for those hot tropical nights.

I was a small town girl that had traveled the States extensively but had never gone overseas until January of 2000 when I was a Goodwill Ambassador for Rotary International. I went to the Philippines for a six-week exchange program. During my first week there, I met my Amiel Brosoto. He was the "International Relations Ambassador" for his Rotary club. He was so sweet! When I called home and told my mom I had met the most wonderful guy – my mom actually knew from my voice that I was in LOVE!

We spent six weeks together – I came home knowing I was going to marry this man. And so, my journey into the "immigration jungle" came to be. After Amiel asked me to marry him, our process to petition him on a fiance visa began. I did some research on the Internet and found an immigration attorney. My mom and I went to meet with her. We both liked her and with her

guidance and expertise, I was able to marry the love of my life. Many Americans don't realize the importance of immigrants. Our society gains so much from these wonderful people and their cultures. I believe it is important for all Americans to realize that at one time we were all immigrants. I hope you enjoy our recipes. The Turon (page 103) is my favorite and my sister-in-law taught me how to make it.

~ by Penny Porter Brosoto

Turon ~ Fried Bananas

By *Penny Porter Brosoto and Amiel Brosoto*

Cut bananas lengthwise. Roll in white or brown sugar. My husband prefers brown sugar because it makes the Turon sweeter.

Place oil in an electric wok (or a regular frying pan) and set to high. Once you have the banana coated in sugar, roll it in the egg roll wrapper and then fry it. Now serve it up!

white or brown sugar

egg roll wrappers

ripe bananas

vegetable oil

See Penny and Amiel's story and photo on page 101.

6 oz bittersweet chocolate

1-1/2 sticks butter

3/4 cup sugar

4 eggs

Fondant au Chocolat

By Laurent and Kathy Denis

Preheat oven to 400° F.

Melt chocolate, butter and sugar in a pan on stove top using medium heat. Let mixture cool slightly, then whisk in eggs, one at a time. Next, pour the result into a quiche or tart pan.

Cook at 400° F for 18 minutes. Take out of the oven and let cool with a plate on top of the dish. When cool, sprinkle with powdered sugar. Serve with raspberry coulis if desired.

See Kathy and Laurent's story on page 54.

Flan with Fresh Berries

By Maria Varchavtchik Imhof and Michael Imhof

Split 1 cup of sugar into 1/3 cup and 2/3 cup measurements. Pour 1/3 cup sugar into a double boiler and cook until it caramelizes. Blend 2/3 sugar with other ingredients above and pour into the caramelized pan.

Cook for at least 30 minutes on low heat on the stove top or in the oven at 350° F until the pudding is firm. When the flan is cooked and firm, flip it upside down onto a plate. Refrigerate after it has cooled.

To make caramel sauce, put a cup of sugar in non-stick frying pan a pan over low heat until it melts and turns a light brown color (caramelizes). Pour on top of cooled flan.

Serve the flan in a nice dish with caramel sauce on top. Add blueberries or strawberries for decoration.

3 eggs

1 (15 oz) can condensed milk

1 can whole milk *use condensed milk can for measure*

2 cups sugar with 1 cup for caramel sauce

1-2 cups fresh berries

Maria grew up in Sorocaba, Brazil. When Maria and her brother Luiz were children, they spent a summer in Kansas as guests of a Pittsburgh State University professor, an old family friend. So when it was time to go to college, Maria chose Pittsburgh State. That's where she met Michael, a native of Southeast Kansas. They would often pass each other on campus; Michael would always take notice of the long, dark-haired beauty. They formally met on a Tuesday night after a university bowling league game. Michael thought Maria was American because her English was flawless. Maria gave Michael her phone number. Michael called several times to set up a date, but Maria's father was visiting for a month, and she could not find the time! One day her father listened to one of Michael's messages. He then said, "Why don't you give a poor sap a chance?" The rest is history.

They met for their first date at Maria's place. Michael cooked her an artichoke and eggplant pizza. Since then, Maria has cooked many tasty things for Michael, and she is an amazingly good cook. She once made this flan recipe for a student party. A student from Turkey ate a piece and said that the flan was so good, he was interested in marrying Maria. That's when Michael realized it was time to act, pronto. Michael and Maria are now married. Despite being in love and having a lot of fun in college, Maria finished her Bachelor's degree in Marketing and Michael finished his Master's in Finance.

They now live in Texas, where Michael is working on a PhD in International Finance and Maria works in marketing.

1 cup walnuts *chopped finely, with some left whole*

1 cup almonds *chopped finely, with some left whole*

Honey *to taste*

Go Nuts!

By Anand Nagarajan and Miryana Lazarevic

Dry roast the nuts in a pan on low heat for 5 - 10 minutes, stir to avoid burning. Remove the nuts from the pan and place into a bowl. Mix the honey into the nuts and let cool to room temperature. Refrigerate for 10 minutes to chill to taste.

Go Nuts is a quick fix dessert that we often make. It is an original as far as we know. These nuts are our favorite combination. However, you may also want to try other nuts. Instead of honey you can also try maple syrup or molasses or chocolate syrup or a combination of these. Go ahead, experiment … we did!

Photo provided by Anand Nagarajan and Miryana Lazarevic

Anand is from Chennai, India. Miryana is from Belgrade, Serbia. They met at the Frankfurt airport, a classic case of love at first sight. Miryana was fascinated with the Indian culture and looked forward to moving to India, but that didn't work because her health suffered there. Anand was fascinated with Miryana, so he moved to Serbia but it didn't work either because he did not speak Serbian well enough to settle there. Anand had spent time in the U.S. on business and

thought they should try the great American melting pot for as their future home. It worked. Through the transition from being individuals from different cultures to being partners living in a third country, Anand and Miryana have been enjoying the life's journey. They have many good friends in their new world. They currently live in Southern California where they enjoy the mild weather and spectacular sunsets.

Brigadeiros ~ Brazilian Bon Bons (continued from page 88)

I also earned a Doctorate in Education, Urban Leadership and Policy Studies. Today, as Director of the English as a Second Language program of the University of Missouri-Kansas City and the Metropolitan Community Colleges of Kansas City, Missouri, I facilitate the integration of the newcomers into our society by providing language instruction. At UMKC, one of my roles is to teach students who are working on their TESOL-related Master's degrees.

It may sound corny, but over and over I feel the need to express my gratitude to my parents who guided me towards a love for education and compassion, to my husband, who is very supportive of me and my best friend, and to my son who gives me a reason to try so hard.

~by Monica Mingucci

Buttercream Cupcakes (continued from page 89)

I knew no Spanish at the time so Sergio tried to help me. I even got one of those little "conversation" Spanish books. One day, he tricked me into asking him to go to the movies. He kept on saying the sentence incorrectly, and I said, "No that's not right. It's 'Will you go to the movies with me?" And then he said "yes!" What a funny guy...

Sergio proposed to me at my 22nd birthday party. He baked a cheesecake with a chocolate box on the top, and inside the box, there was a ring. It was very fitting for him ... being a baker and all. We were married the next year in June and he even made our wedding cake. I was so nervous that he wouldn't get it done and I could only imagine how much work he had to do right up to the last minute. But he made it to the wedding on time and the cake was beautiful. We've been in love ever since.

~ by Allyson Gonzalez

resource guide

While specializing in a particular region, the stores listed below also carry many items from various cultures. For example, India Emporium naturally carries traditional Indian and Pakistani items but you will also find Armenian spices, Bulgarian feta cheese and "life changing" Arabic pickles. Also, categories below are very unscientific: India and the Middle East actually happen to be located in Asia, but I listed them separately thinking that Asian markets probably should include China, Vietnam and Laos. It seems that food can be as complex as life itself, and I hope that my readers go to these stores and discover the exotic tastes and treasures found inside on their own.

AFRICAN

African Tropical Market
901 N 7th Street
Kansas City, Kansas
913.371.0061

ASIAN

Asian Super Market
9538 Nall Avenue
Overland Park, Kansas
913.642.0690

Chinatown Market
202 Grand Boulevard
Kansas City, Missouri
816.472.6363

Hung Vuong Market
1006 E 5th Street
Kansas City, Missouri
816.221.9642

Lao Market
20 South 10th Street
Kansas City, Missouri
913.281.2877

Huong Que Oriental Market
424 Locust Lane
Kansas City, Missouri
816.471.1774

COOKWARE

Pryde's Old Westport
115 Westport Road
Kansas City, Missouri
816.531.5588

FARMER'S MARKETS

City Market
20 E 5th St. #201
Kansas City, Missouri
816.842.1271

Farmer's Community Market
at Brookside
63rd and Wornall Street
Kansas City, Missouri
913.515.2426

Lawrence Farmer's Market
1000 Block of Vermont Street
Lawrence, Kansas
785.331.4445

Merriam Farmer's Market
5740 Merriam Drive
Merriam, Kansas
913.322.5550

INDIAN

India Emporium
10458 Metcalf Avenue
Overland Park, Kansas
913.642.1161

Ambica Foods
9054 Metcalf Avenue
Overland Park, Kansas
913.901.8700

Patel Foods
7214 119th and Metcalf Avenue
Overland Park, Kansas
913.696.1950

IRISH/BRITISH

Brits
929 Massachusetts Street
Lawrence, Kansas
785.843.2288

Browne's Irish Market
3300 Pennsylvania Avenue
Kansas City, Missouri
816.561.0030

Sheehan's Irish Market
412 Westport Road
Kansas City, Missouri
816.561.4480

ITALIAN

Marco Polo's Italian Market
201 West 103rd Street
Kansas City, Missouri
816.941.6600

LATIN AMERICAN

Latin-O-Market
10452 Metcalf Avenue
Overland Park, Kansas
913.381.1704

La Mexicana Market
848 Central Avenue
Kansas City, Kansas
913.621.7462

Abarrotes Y Tortilleria Mexico
806 Southwest Blvd
Kansas City, Missouri
816.842.0160

Bazar Latino
1208 E Santa Fe Street
Olathe, Kansas
913.829.6567

MIDDLE-EASTERN

Alhabashi Mart (River Market)
311 Main Street
Kansas City, Missouri
816.421.6727

Aladdin Café
1021 Massachusetts Street
Lawrence, Kansas
785.832.1100

Mediterranean Market
7417 Metcalf Avenue #B
Overland Park, Kansas
913.722.7744

Mediterranean Market and Café
3300 W 15th Street #B5
Lawrence, Kansas
785.842.9383

INTERNATIONAL

Euro Market
6942 N Oak Trafficway
Kansas City, Missouri
816.436-8331

International Grocery
7228 W 79th Street
Shawnee Mission, Kansas
913.385.5609

International Market,
10328 Mastin Street
Overland Park, Kansas
913.438.3663

The Community Mercantile
901 Iowa Street
Lawrence, Kansas
785.843.8544

Wheatfields
904 Vermont Street
Lawrence, Kansas
785.841.5553